CW01457680

Studies in the Illustration of the Psalter

ST ANDREWS STUDIES IN THE HISTORY OF ART

STUDIES
in the
ILLUSTRATION
of the
PSALTER

Edited by

BRENDAN CASSIDY

and

ROSEMARY MUIR WRIGHT

SHAUN TYAS

STAMFORD

2000

© The Contributors, 2000

Typeset from the disc of the editors
by the publisher

Published by

SHAUN TYAS
18, Adelaide Street
Stamford
Linbcolnshire
PE9 2EN

Published in Association with
The School of Art History
University of St Andrews

ISBN
1 900289 42 3

Printed and bound in the United Kingdom by the Alden Group, Oxford

CONTENTS

PREFACE

The present volume contains the papers presented at a symposium on the illumination of the medieval Psalter that was held in St Andrews in May 1997. On that occasion Lucy Freeman Sandler from the University of New York was invited to give the Saunders Lecture; an annual lecture organized by the School of Art History and funded from a bequest of O. E. Saunders. Octavia Elfrida Saunders, a distinguished medievalist and former student of St Andrews, wrote one of the earliest surveys in English of medieval manuscript illumination and so it was particularly fitting that Professor Sandler chose as her theme, the illustration of late-medieval English psalters. Given the current interest in the psalter, this suggested to us the possibility of convening a gathering of other scholars whose interests complemented Professor Sandler's. She encouraged us in our plans.

It was not intended that the symposium should be encyclopaedic in its sweep. Our aims were modest. We hoped for a range of papers, various in approach and examining manuscripts of varying dates and provenance, that would add to the store of knowledge of how artists responded to this most fascinating Biblical text. In this we were not disappointed. Speakers ranged in their coverage from the eighth to the fourteenth century. And although the balance of emphasis was on illuminated psalters produced in the British Isles, there were not infrequent forays abroad. Most gratifyingly, some of our speakers revisited some of the most celebrated books ever produced, including the Book of Kells and the Utrecht Psalter. To all our contributors we owe a profound thanks not only for their endeavours towards making the conference the scholarly and social success that it was but for the (generally) prompt and good-humoured way in which they responded to their often importunate editors.

Others are deserving of our gratitude, both for their contributions to the conference and their help in the preparation of the text for publication. To two consecutive heads of the School of Art History, Graham Smith and Peter Humfrey, we are grateful not only for their support of our efforts but also for their readiness to allocate the funds necessary to make the project a success. Christine Linnell and Suzanne Lyle, quondam graduate students, were enthusiastic, conscientious and helpful in myriad ways at the conference and the former provided invaluable editorial assistance in preparing the volume ready for the press.

LIST OF ILLUSTRATIONS

2. Corbie Psalter, Psalm 31. Amiens, Bibl. municipale MS 18, fol. 26v (photo: Bibl. municipale)
3. Corbie Psalter, Psalm 57. Amiens, Bibl. municipale MS 18, fol. 50v (photo: Bibl. municipale)
4. Book of Kells. Dublin, Trinity Coll. MS A.I.6, fol. 122r (photo: Trinity Coll.)
5. Corbie Psalter, Psalm 9. Amiens, Bibl. municipale MS 18, fol. 7v (photo: Bibl. municipale)
6. Corbie Psalter, Psalm 72. Amiens, Bibl. municipale MS 18, fol. 101r (photo: Bibl. municipale)
7. Corbie Psalter, Psalm 108. Amiens, Bibl. municipale MS 18, fol. 92v (photo: Bibl municipale)
8. Corbie Psalter, Psalm 61. Amiens, Bibl. municipale MS 18, fol. 53r (photo: Bibl. municipale)

Noel

1. Psalm 39. Baltimore, Walters Art Gallery MS W.88, fol. 150v (photo: Walters Art Gall.)
2. Annunciation. Baltimore, Walters Art Gallery MS W.82, fol. 171r (photo: Walters Art Gall.)
3. Utrecht Psalter, Canticle of Habbakuk. Utrecht, Rijksuniversiteit Bibl. MS 32, fol 85v (detail) (photo: Rijksuniversiteit Bibl.)
4. Utrecht Psalter, Psalm 108. Utrecht, Rijksuniversiteit Bibl. MS 32, fol. 64r (detail) (photo: Rijksuniversiteit Bibl.)
5. Utrecht Psalter, Psalm 21. Utrecht, Rijksuniversiteit Bibl. MS 32, fol. 12r (detail) (photo: Rijksuniversiteit Bibl.)
6. London, British Lib. MS Cotton Titus D.xxvii, fol. 75v. (photo: British Lib.)

Kidd

1. London, British Lib. MS Arundel 60, fol. 12v (photo: Courtauld Institute, Conway Library)
2. London, British Lib. MS Arundel 60, fol. 52v (photo: Courtauld Institute, Conway Library)
3. London, British Lib. MS Arundel 60, fol. 11v (photo: Courtauld Institute, Conway Library)

Backhouse

1. Burdett Psalter-Hours. Private Collection, fol. 76r (photo: the author)
2. Burdett Psalter-Hours. Private Collection, fol. 8v (photo: the author)
3. Burdett Psalter-Hours. Private Collection, fol. 9r (photo: the author)
4. Burdett Psalter-Hours. Private Collection, fol. 10v (photo: the author)

Introducing the Medieval Psalter

ROSEMARY MUIR WRIGHT

In the Medieval West, the poetry of the psalms was the well-spring of Christian worship, both in community and in private. In words so familiar as to lodge in the memory and so evocative as to touch the extremes of human feeling, the voice of the psalmist speaks in a language of intimacy with God, in words of despair, protest, supplication and thanksgiving. The vivid imagery of this poetry invited visual expression. Whatever the period, the illustration of the Psalter could be seen as responding imaginatively to the needs and aspirations of the reader/listener to give focus to the personal nature of the prayer of the psalm. 'The visualisation of the psalm text in concrete, factual terms reinforced the authority of the biblical text and stressed the notion that the words of the Bible were literally true.'[1] The psalms themselves may have been created over seven centuries from as early as the tenth century B.C. and some may indeed date from the time of David who was considered to be their author. The medieval belief in David as the writer of the psalms charged them with special resonance. David, an ancestor and prefiguration of Christ, was born of a royal lineage uniquely favoured by God.

As a book for all seasons and for all conditions of men and women, the psalter has been used as the prayer book of the Church from the time of Augustine to that of Bonhoeffer. Despite its source in the Old Testament, the Book of Psalms was interpreted by the early Church in a Christological sense in which the psalms were regarded as both the prayers of Christ himself and as prayers addressed to him.[2] In addition, by the fourth century, the psalms were regarded as the official voice of the Church. Because of their essential musical quality, the rise and fall of their cadences, the psalm verses lent themselves to chant or melody. These cadences were prompted by the psalms'

[1]   The Utrecht Psalter in Medieval Art, Picturing the Psalms of David, K. van der Horst, W. Noel, and W. C. M. Wüstefeld (eds), MS't Goy and London 1996, p. 55.
[2]   The Church at Prayer. An Introduction to the Liturgy: iv, The Liturgy and Time, A. G. Martimort, J. H. Dalmais and P. Jounel (eds), London 1986, p. 193, where it is noted that the word kyros meaning Lord was interpreted as referring to Christ by the early Fathers such as Tertullian and Origen.

1

poetic language in which rhythm, metaphor and repetition evoked sound patterns which could readily be used in worship. Reciting the psalms, with their variety of phrasing and of mood, encouraged the division of the verses into answering voices which gathered the community into one. From the fourth century, the psalms were organised into a routine of communal prayer to form a liturgy of the hours. The old habit of morning and evening prayer (derived from Jewish practice) was fused with the monastic cycle which adopted the continuous reading of the psalter over a certain period of time. This time span was later formalised by the sixth-century Rule of St Benedict as being the space of one week. The choice of psalm grouping by which the 150 canonical psalms were all recited weekly, was dictated in part by their textual appropriateness to morning or evening prayer. In addition the christological interpretation of the psalms meant that certain psalms were particularly significant at specific points in the liturgical year. Certain psalms because of their content were grouped together as the Penitential Psalms and were to play a central part in the process of penance, being recited daily after prime in monastic use and during Lent in secular use. On the other hand, the Gradual Psalms as psalms invoking trust in God's aid were those sung daily before Matins in monastic use and during Advent and Lent only, in secular use. St Benedict's Rule had as its aim a balanced and workable synthesis of the existing forms of the liturgy of the hours, and his division, while intended only for his own monastery at Monte Cassino, was generally adopted to become the *Opus Dei* of Western monasticism.[3] This formulation of groups of psalms to be said or sung on different days of the week and at different times of the day, marked the passage of time throughout the liturgical year, as well as the changes in daylight through sunrise to sunset and protected the praying community by continuing through the hours of darkness, which for many could also mean the hours of death.

The text of the psalter could be one of two kinds. The most straightforward was the biblical psalter which was a single book extracted from the Bible, containing the canonical psalms in numerical order but divided into five sections beginning at Psalms 1, 41, 72, 89 and 106.[4] Examples survive from as early as the sixth century, suggesting the need to extrapolate this book of the Bible into a separate volume intended for study or prayer. Because the language of the psalms was ambiguously poetic, the text offered opportunities for interpretation. The existence of marginal or interlinear

[3] R. Taft, *The Liturgy of the Hours in East and West*, Collegeville, Minnesota 1986, pp. 121–40. The Benedictine divisions for the Roman monastic office were based on the old Rule of the Master and the Roman Office of Benedict's own day. By contrast, the Irish monastic cursus imposed a staggering burden of psalms during the three night offices especially in winter, pp. 114–5.

[4] A. Hughes, *Medieval Manuscripts for Mass and Office. A Guide to Their Organization and Terminology*, Toronto 1982, p. 225.

glosses on these psalter manuscripts bears witness to their use as texts for meditation and study.

The second type of psalter was the liturgical psalter which differed from its biblical counterpart in providing additional material for the performances of the daily services. Instead of the psalms following on, one after the other, as they do in their Old Testament location, here they were grouped in sequences by the days of the week (*per ferias*) in keeping with the offices of the church year and those of the saints. The sequence was determined by the time of their recitation on the different days of the week and at the canonical hours of the day.[5] As this sequential arrangement was determined by their liturgical use, additional material was often added to help in the performance of the Divine Office. The musical quality of the psalms was emphasised by the addition of trinitarian doxologies at the end of each of the five groups of psalms of the Vulgate arrangement, for example, 'gloria patri et filio et spiritu sancto in saecula saeculorum'. Such a doxology was useful both as a closure to the psalm and as a reminder of its Christological aspect, necessary because of the psalm's Jewish origin.[6] Antiphons were added to be sung as refrains and so they too acquired a musical form. Their rhythm and melody also ensured that they would be easily memorised. To assist in the Christian interpretation of the psalms titles were given to them of which as many as ten series still exist in manuscripts.[7] Where the psalm title imposed a Christological or ecclesiastical gloss indicating how the words could be interpreted from the perspective of the New Testament, the Psalter Collect summarised the content of a particular psalm in the form of a prayer repeated after the psalm itself.[8] All these additions were intended to assist in the praying of the psalms

[5]   The psalter thus became part of the Breviary which contained all the offices for the public liturgy of the church prepared for both monastic and for secular use. Although the weekly recitation of the entire 150 psalms was common to both breviary offices, the distribution of the psalms was different. The eight-part liturgical division of the secular or choir psalter was 1, 26, 38, 51, 52, 68, 80, 97, 109 (Vulgate numeration) and had a cycle which began at matins on Sunday with the first psalm and then proceeded through Monday to Saturday, beginning with psalms 26, 38, 52, 68, 80 and 97 respectively, while psalm 109 was the first psalm for Sunday Vespers. In the monastic psalter there was no division at psalms 80 and 97.

[6]   See Hughes 1982 (as n. 4 above), p. 24.

[7]   See *The Church at Prayer* 1985 (as n. 2 above), p. 203. For example, the title of Psalm 34, *Judica Domine, nocentes me* ('Judge thou, O Lord, them that wrong me'), reinforces the Christological connection as follows, 'David, in the person of Christ, prayeth against his persecutors: prophetically foreshewing the punishments that shall fall upon them'. See *The Holy Bible translated from the Latin Vulgate, and diligently compared with other editions in divers languages, Douay, A.D. 1609: Rheims, A.D. 1582,* London 1914.

[8]   *The Psalter Collects, from V–VIth-Century Sources,* Dom L. Brou (ed.) London

3

and clearly signalled the practical necessity of having a separate, easily referenced volume, known as the Breviary.

The Latin text of the psalms existed in several recensions of which the three most important were associated with Jerome. His first revision of 382–85 A.D. derived from a number of Latin translations of the psalms circulating in Rome in the fourth century. A second revision as part of a review of the entire Bible was made soon afterwards, between 386 and 387 A.D. This was intended as a scholarly edition, supported as it was by a manuscript of Origen's *Hexapla* in the library at Caesarea. Despite the fact that this revision was not intended for use in the liturgy, it is the version which overtook all other Latin psalter texts for use in the Mass and Divine Office from the ninth century. Its appropriation for liturgical use may have been instigated by its independent survival as the only part of the original biblical revision of 386–87. A third biblical revision of 392–93 A.D. from the basic Hebrew text produced a third version which was used only where the different texts of the psalms were set in parallel for study purposes.

The original lay-out of the psalm text had been affected by the major changes that had taken place in the writing of the Bible as a whole. Within the compilation of the biblical books, the Book of Psalms shared in changes of script, the separation of words and the introduction of modulated punctuation common to the other books. These conventions also applied to the Book of Psalms when written as a separate volume. Each psalm would be clearly distinguished by a larger initial, operating as a marker and as a text break. This opening initial immediately became the site of distinctive decoration which developed into a visual signal of the actual contents of the psalm itself. Each verse would be given a new line and changes in pitch and breath points marked. This represented the minimum setting for the scribe. The repetitive patterns of lines and spaces meant that sections of script could be clearly differentiated and 'read'.

This clarity of access was crucial for the cleric who was required to sing the psalms from memory, especially during the night offices and for their formal reading in the refectory or in the choir. The size of volumes may give some indication of their use as may the extent and siting of their decoration. The daily exposure to the words of the psalms in the eight liturgical hours of each monastic day ensured their imprint on the memory especially when the recitation of each individual monk was echoed by the voices of his fellows. In the dark silences of the night offices, in the grey dawn of the returning day and in the shadowing of the evening hours, the performance of the psalms was constant, affirming the unfailing certainty of the Divine ordering beyond the accidental circumstances of time and place.

1949.

But oral repetition alone would not be sufficient to ensure that the psalms were committed to memory. There was the additional requirement that they should be read. This had huge consequences for the manner in which the text was decorated and indeed the extent and quality of the visual illustration demonstrates how responsive psalter illustration was to the the needs of the reader. From the early Middle Ages, the psalter served a dual purpose, as a prayer book and as a primer for learning letters.[9] As the psalms were recognised by their opening words and not their numbers, the letters which formed those words had to be clearly recognisable and understood. From the seventh to the ninth century, these opening words were heralded by an illustrated initial, infilled with stylised animal patterns, trumpet spirals and interlace. However the inhabited initial, in which a figure or figures occupies the space of the letter, became especially popular in the tenth and eleventh centuries. Bernard Meehan's paper illustrates both these phenomena in the precocious illustration of the Corbie Psalter (Amiens, Bibl. municipale MS 18) of about 800, where the bounding edge of the letter shape is transformed into the expressive contours of figures evoked by the content of the psalm itself. By the twelfth century, this figuration had developed into a pictorial narrative or allegorical scene which tended to overwhelm the shape of the letter or to marginalise it to a framing device for the pictorial infill. In this process, the opening initial which had been bonded to the words of the text, so clearly demonstrated in the Irish practice of diminuendo, became increasingly separated from the other letters and the picture took over the role of highlighting the particular psalm.

More dramatic than the focus on the initial was the insertion of full or half page miniatures which marked important parts of the text or signalled a reflective pause in the reading process. From the earliest tradition of psalter illustration such illustration had occurred at specified points in the book. The old tripartite division in the eighth-century copy of Cassiodorus' Commentary on the Psalms (Durham, Cathedral Lib. MS B.II 30) would have been marked originally by three full-page miniatures at the opening of psalms 1, 51 and 101. The earliest surviving illustrated psalter, the Vespasian Psalter produced at St Augustine's Abbey, Canterbury in the second quarter of the eighth century (London, British Lib. MS Cotton Vespasian A.1), may have had pictures at these same divisions, in addition to a carpet page set between the text of the psalms and the canticles. In this case the misplaced historiated initial of David and his musicians probably signalled the opening of Psalm 1.

---

[9]   E. Bishop, 'On the Origin of the Prymer', in *Liturgica Historica*, Oxford 1918, pp. 231–47 where he points out that the word primer is a reflection of the word for the office of Prime, said every morning. See also C. de Hamel, *A History of Illuminated Manuscripts*, London 1994, p.12. Details of how the psalter was used in the development of lay literacy are found in M. Clanchy, *From Memory to Written Record, England 1066–1307*, Cambridge, MA 1979, repr. 1993, pp. 191–6.

A more extensive type of illustration, however, was the inclusion of prefatory miniatures designed to link the psalms with the New Testament through the pictured cycles of the life of Christ and later, the Virgin. By the twelfth century, this pictorial narrative effectively embedded the events of Christ's life in the liturgical offices of the Christian year. Clearly the selection of these narrative scenes could have a bearing on the function of the text and further demonstrate the flexibility of the illustrative potential of the psalter. It is clear from the additions to the psalm text, the calendar, litany and petitioner's prayers for example, that the psalter functioned in the daily life of the owner and that this owner need not be a cleric. Indeed some of the most famous illuminated psalters were made for lay people of high status. As a primer for reading skills, the psalter found its place in aristocratic households. From as early as the eighth century, the secular psalter also served as a prayer book in the hands of a readership that had claims to at least a minimum level of literacy. To read meant to have direct access to the words of the sacred texts and although complete understanding may only have been achieved with the guidance of a confessor or chaplain, the potential for individual apprehension was enormous. Stimulated by the images, lay readers might apply the words of the psalm to their own present circumstances and the intimate language of the poetry ensured immediate access to the Divine.

In addition to the prefatory cycles, the opening words of the first psalm often received a full page illustration in which the initial 'B' of the word *beatus* was so magnified as to dominate the text folio to the point of providing an internal pictorial field for elaborate decoration encased in the swelling contours of the letter. It functioned as a visual marker for the opening of the psalms and offered a double field for pictorial exegesis separated by the central bar of the letter. The elaborated 'B' of the assertive 'Blessed is the man...' became the most distinctive feature of the decoration of the psalter, a hallmark of both its textual content and its lexical potential.

Apart from the distinctive feature of the Beatus page the iconography of psalter decoration is difficult to categorise given the diversity of contexts in which the psalter was used. However some general points can be made in the light of the detailed studies by Sandler, Noel and Backhouse. Faced with the task of illustrating psalm verses, designers and artists could call on an artistic tradition governed by two dominant themes, those of authorship and word pictures. Drawing on the medieval belief in David as author of the psalms, the assertive presence of the Old Testament king could dominate the illustrations both in the opening sequence in the form of an author portrait and in the narrative episodes from his life, which marked the opening initials of the liturgical divisions and the marginal spaces of Gothic manuscripts. In many instances, these familiar biblical episodes were used to illustrate the trials of the Christian life. David's struggle against the armoured might of the giant Goliath could be read as an example of Christian fortitude against evil.

David's unction as king by Samuel gave sanction to claims for royal anointing and the ideal of the monarch as priest and exalted servant.[10] David's contrition after his adultery with Bathsheba was an appropriate theme for the opening of the Penitential Psalms, while David as a musician was a constant visual reminder of the sound quality of the verses and the continuity of the church at prayer. In addition, the significance of the lineage of David shared by the earthly parents of Christ invited the adaptation of the iconographic theme of the Tree of Jesse sometimes as a single frontispiece miniature as in the Ormesby and St. Omer Psalters (Oxford, Bodleian Lib. MS Douce 366; London, British Lib. MS Add. 39810) of the first quarter of the fourteenth century.[11] The focus on the humanity of Christ stimulated by the debates over Transubstantiation which preceded the Fourth Lateran Council of 1215, encouraged the inclusion of imagery from the life of the Virgin in the prefatory cycles of the twelfth century. After 1215 the extent of the devotion to the Virgin led to the development of a sequence of offices known as the Hours of the Blessed Virgin Mary. These offices incorporating the psalms of the liturgical hours slowly developed from the mid-thirteenth century into a different type of devotional prayer book, the Book of Hours.

The St Andrews symposium was designed to reveal aspects of the historical evolution of the psalter's decoration and to highlight some of the problematic areas of interpretation. It seemed valuable to bring those discussions together in a single volume as the illustrated psalter has been neglected compared with its successor, the books of hours. Yet it is in the illustration of the psalter that so much has been clarified about the relationship between text and its decoration, both major and minor. Inherent in the poetic nature of the psalms is their evocation of word pictures, images generated by the literal illustration of specific words or parts of words lately described as '*imagines verborum*'. This can be demonstrated in the earliest of the manuscripts here discussed, the Corbie Psalter, whose tissue-fine leaves barely support the fading spectacle of its distinctly classicising initial decoration. The common palaeographic links and zoomorphic elements between Corbie and the Book of Kells is noted by Bernard Meehan whose exploration of the correspondences between the illustration of the two manuscripts opens up discussion concerning the meaning of the discs above the profile figures on fol.123v of Kells by linking them to the discs in the Corbie Psalter initials where, as a cross within a roundel, they recall the imagery of Christ. In his paper he draws attention to the manner in which the example in the Corbie psalter presents its themes in

---

[10]   R. Deshman, 'The Exalted Servant. The Ruler Theology of the Prayer Book of Charles the Bold', *Viator* 2, 1980, pp. 385–417.

[11]   L. F. Sandler, *Gothic Manuscripts 1285–1385* (A Survey of Manuscripts Illuminated in the British Isles, J. J. G. Alexander [ed.], vol. 5), London 1986, vol. 2, pp. 49–51 and 113–5.

an unambiguous manner in comparison to the allusive references of the Kells gospel book. He points out the range of models which must have been available to the artists of Kells, who adapted the imagery of contemporary manuscripts to their own purposes. Just what these purposes might have been is suggested by Heather Pulliam's paper which analyses the use of the zoomorphic decoration in the Corbie Psalter in relation to the actual words of the adjacent text to demonstrate that even secondary decorative features are being used exegetically. In particular she isolates the motif of entanglement and self-ensnarement and relates it to Augustine's Commentary on the Psalms, of which a multi-volume copy was produced at Corbie itself. For example, Pulliam demonstrates how the imagery of the Corbie Psalter makes plain the Augustinian distinction between 'falling' and 'being fallen' as a description of man's state. The voice of the commentary must have shaped and given focus to the imagery of the individual psalms in ways not easily accessible to our contemporary viewing habits. However, the words of the commentary act not only to expand the meaning of the image but also to delimit the boundaries of interpretation. The appearance of such imagery at this early date may have been provoked by the need to control the readership lest too 'open' a reading of the visual features should lead to misinterpretation of the psalter's text. The consistency which Pulliam notices in the use of these visual details of the decorative repertoire to enunciate the vocabulary of the psalm text suggests that the Corbie Psalter, and incidentally the Book of Kells itself, articulates what she refers to as 'a language of ornament, now lost'.

The distinction between the actual vocabulary of images and their syntax is discussed in William Noel's paper on the Utrecht Psalter which is one of the most famous of Carolingian manuscripts written at Hautvilliers, near Rheims in about 830. Again he stresses the essential difference in the type of illustration required for a poetic text like the psalter, compared to those demanded by the narratives of other biblical texts. He warns that the Utrecht Psalter contains illustrations, not of events, but of individual words. Conventional narrative principles do not apply to the illustration of the psalms even when the images are unified visually by extended landscape settings. Noel subsitutes the idea of 'charade illustration' for the phrase 'literal illustration' implied by the term *imagines verborum*. This charade parallel allows him to demonstrate how the images of Utrecht may illustrate not only particular phrases or words from the psalm but even syllables of words used out of their textual context. He stresses that contrary to our contemporary expectations, visual proximity within the Utrecht images is more likely to be metaphorical in intention, meaning 'like' rather than 'next to' and that this distinction in the visual syntax is extremely sophisticated. It implies a literate culture used to playing on the differences between words and pictures and able to assemble a fluent combination of images which then need to be broken up into discrete units before their verbal equivalents can be grasped.

Close attention to the details of the pen work of the scribe is the hallmark of Peter Kidd's paper which deals with the significance of a small red cross inscribed in the Easter Table of MS Arundel 60, an eleventh-century psalter from Winchester. His treatment of this scribal notation provides a realistic date for the production of the manuscript and its possible owner, Riwallon, abbot of the New Minster. The paper cautions against the simplistic notion that any manuscript with 'Anglo-Saxon' decoration and Old English glosses must necessarily pre-date the Norman Conquest. As proof of the need for caution, Peter Kidd reminds us that Cotton Caligula A.xv is a post-Conquest production despite its Anglo-Saxon decoration and Old English text, just like the 'relentlessly Anglo-Saxon' Cotton Tiberius C.vi, dated with certainty after 1064 and probably after 1066 itself. His careful attention to the script, ruling and quire collation of the Arundel Psalter suggests that there were two scribes working more or less contemporaneously in the decade after the Conquest.

The identification of hands is also a feature of Janet Backhouse's paper on the thirteenth-century Burdett-Psalter Hours, reproductions of which we were privileged to see for the first time in public. Apart from the delight of seeing a newly discovered manuscript, brought for comment to the British Library some twenty years ago, it is a useful example of a type of personal devotional text in which both the psalter and the Hours of the Virgin are bound within one book, a type that was extremely popular in the late thirteenth and early fourteenth century on both sides of the Channel. In the case of the Burdett-Psalter Hours, Janet Backhouse has established that the miniatures were likely to have been done by the principal court illuminator in Paris, known as the Melician Master. The owner was a Hospitaller, illustrated both as a suppliant at the feet of John the Baptist on a single full-page leaf and four times more as a marginal figure at major text divisions. Despite being produced in a Paris workshop however, the text of the Hours of the Virgin follows the Use of Sarum and commemorative entries added to the calendar before 1300 point to an English owner, possibly Joseph de Chauncy, Prior of the Hospitallers (1273–80) and Treasurer to Edward I. The paper scrupulously follows the possible line of descent of this manuscript until it came into the hands of the Burdett family and provides an insight into the maze of possible ownership and family connections. This book is provided with a full cycle of illustrations common to the book of hours and in some way reflective of the prefatory miniatures of the psalter which similarly identified the salient moments of the New Testament narrative in anticipation of the psalm text itself, signalling its christological interpretation.

The continued viability of the literal mode of psalter illustration into the thirteenth and fourteenth centuries is demonstrated in Lucy Freeman Sandler's paper which describes this system as one used almost solely in connection with the pictorial strategies of medieval psalters. She describes how the words of the psalm, nouns and verbs, were used metaphorically and turned into images in what Sandler describes as 'a pictorial acting out' which was designed to stimulate the reader to engage with the text in order to find an explanation for the images. This activity of looking, searching and reading is particularly evident in cases like the Luttrell Psalter where there are marginal images. She demonstrates how the text is made visually relevant by pictorial images which may even disregard the spirit of the psalm to invent pictorial equivalents from contemporary life. For example, in the Luttrell Psalter, the reference to 'works of the hands of men' was illustrated by the labours which went into the preparation and presentation of the lord's feast rather than into the creation of idols. Sandler stresses that the disengagement of word images from their context is the explanation for the invention of complex images found only in Gothic psalters with marginal illustrations. As an example, she shows convincingly how this decontextualisation provokes the hybrids and the mock narratives of the Luttrell Psalter. However, it is clear from the evidence which she offers that word images are not alike in the ways in which they are related to the text. She examines the ways in which transpositions of words into images intersect with the physical format of the psalter. In the horizontal layout of the Paris Psalter for example, the visual compositions encapsulate the whole of the psalm written below, albeit made up of discrete units which refer to different word pictures. The fluidity of the speech scrolls between these units guides the reader's understanding, section by section. By contrast, the historiated initial as an image embedded in the text itself, is usually associated with the opening verse or verses of each psalm. With the marginal imagery, however, a different strategy is adopted as the words do not stand in close physical relation to the image by which they may be interpreted. In this case the word pictures are part of the marginal field rather than the text field. But even there, they are not allowed to float free. The words still exert an invisible control in that the key words or syllables are to be found in the first or last lines on a page, in which position they attract attention quite disproportionate to their verbal importance. The assumption of decontextualization in treating the illustration of the margins ensures the search for the source word from within the text, then as now. This implies that not only the reader but also the artist 'saw' the word acted out in images. Not only does Sandler raise the issue of the way in which text/image relationships functioned but she also raises questions about the literacy of the artist operating in both Latin and Anglo-Norman French. The subtlety with which such decontextualised images are used suggests a level of reading and word exchange which must betray something of the creative process of the illustrator. This also involves questions of the transmission of these images and Sandler has suggested evidence in verbal instructions to the artists from manuscripts from across the Channel, while allowing for the scarcity of English evidence of this kind.

INTRODUCING THE MEDIEVAL PSALTER

The papers in this volume show how the decisions taken about the nature of the illustrations, the intentions of the patron and the social context of the recipient influenced the way in which the familiar words of the psalms were seen as reflecting the hopes and fears of the book's readership. Committed to memory and evoked through imaginative images, the words of the psalms had a life beyond that of the vellum page, in the prayer of the heart.

The Book of Kells and the Corbie Psalter
(with a Note on Harley 2788)

BERNARD MEEHAN

A group of manuscripts produced in northern France in the second half of the eighth century and the beginning of the ninth century has long been recognised as containing elements of script and decoration which draw on a diversity of Byzantine, Merovingian and Insular sources, the latter influence deriving from Irish missionary activity in the area from the sixth century onwards. The Corbie Psalter (Amiens, Bibl. municipale MS 18),[1] produced around the year 800, is an important member of the group, along with the Gellone Sacramentary (Paris, Bibl. nationale MS lat. 12048); Poitiers, Bibl. municipale MS 17; the Stuttgart Psalter (Stuttgart, Württembergische Landesbibl. MS bibl. fol. 23); a decorated text of St Augustine (Paris, Bibl. nationale MS lat. 12168) which Porcher considered was made in imitation of

---

[1] The Corbie psalter contains the Gallican version of the psalter, followed by Canticles (those of Exodus and Habbakuk giving the old and the new version). Additions are made in praise of the Emperor, and can thus be dated later than 800; see J. Porcher, 'L'Evangéliaire de Charlemagne et le psautier d'Amiens', *Revue des Arts* 7, 1957, pp. 50–8. D. Ganz, *Corbie in the Carolingian Renaissance* (Beihefte der Francia, 2), Sigmaringen 1990, p. 133 provides a description and secondary references. For Ganz the artist of Amiens 18 was the artist who worked on Paris, Bibl. nationale MS lat. 13025, which, like Amiens 18, has 'superb and unique figured initials', while that artist also worked on but did not finish Paris, Bibl. nationale MS lat. 4884. See also P. Harbison, *The High Crosses of Ireland. An Iconographical and Photographic Survey*, 3 vols, Bonn 1992, vol. I, pp. 320–1 for comparisons between the Corbie Psalter and Irish crosses; M. Werner, 'Crucifixi, Sepulti, Suscitati .....', *The Book of Kells. Proceedings of a Conference at Trinity College, Dublin, 6–9 September 1992*, F. O'Mahony (ed.), Dublin 1994, p. 487; U. Kuder, 'Die Initialen des Amienspsalter (Amiens, Bibliothèque municipale MS 18)', Ph.D. diss., Ludwig-Maximilians-Universität, Munich 1977. My thanks are due to the Bibliothèque municipale d'Amiens, in particular to Mons. Jean Vilbas, Conservateur des fonds anciens, for permitting study of the Corbie Psalter in June 1994 and for permission to reproduce the accompanying plates from the manuscript. Acknowledgement is made to The Board of Trinity College, Dublin for permission to reproduce comparative images from the Book of Kells.

the style of an insular gospel book; and Paris, Bibl. nationale MS lat. 13159, many of the initials of which were, in E. A. Lowe's words, 'manifestly copied from insular models'.[2] It is not clear whether the Corbie Psalter was produced at Corbie itself or at a neighbouring house.[3] The monastery at Corbie was founded in the middle of the seventh century with monks from Luxeuil, one of St Columbanus's first foundations in Europe after he left Bangor, Co. Down. Corbie remained, as Ganz has noted, 'an important stopping point for travellers to and from the British Isles, as the lives of the Irish saints confirm',[4] while other Irish contacts with northern France were centred on the nearby monasteries of Péronne, founded by St Fursa in the seventh century, and St Riquier (Centula).[5]

As long ago as 1939, Micheli remarked that certain of the zoomorphic motifs of the Corbie Psalter 'composées de quadrupèdes entrelacés au corps étiré, sont d'inspiration insulaire',[6] while in 1967 Françoise Henry noticed the strong Byzantine connections and influence of these manuscripts and their decorative combination of 'the Merovingian fashion of fish-and-bird initials ... with obsessive insular traditions imposing the use of interlacings, animal interlacings and a certain tendency to abstract decoration'.[7] In her 1974 study of the Book of Kells, Henry drew attention to specific decorative features which the Corbie Psalter shares with the Book of Kells, concluding that the

[2]   *Codices Latini Antiquiores*, E. A. Lowe (ed.), Pt. V. France: Paris, Oxford 1950, p. 38, no. 652; J. Porcher, 'La peinture provinciale (régions occidentales)', *Karl der Grosse. Lebenswerk und Nachleben. Band III. Karolingische Kunst*, W. Braunfels and H. Schnitzler (eds), Dusseldorf 1965, pp. 59–61.

[3]   See Porcher 1957 (as n. 1 above), p. 54.

[4]   Ganz 1990 (as n. 1 above), p. 41.

[5]   For the background see F. Henry, *Irish Art during the Viking Invasions: 800–1020 AD*, London 1967, pp. 39–40; F. Henry, *The Book of Kells: Reproductions from the Manuscript in Trinity College, Dublin*, London 1974, pp. 215–8; Ganz 1990 (as n. 1 above), p. 15; B. Bischoff, *Manuscripts and Libraries in the Age of Charlemagne* (Cambridge Studies in Palaeography and Codicology, 1), Cambridge 1994, p. 27; Porcher 1957 (as n. 1 above), p. 55.

[6]   G. L. Micheli, *L'Enluminure de haut moyen âge et les influences irlandaises*, Brussels 1939, p. 86. She continues, '... de longs animaux liés entre eux par des entrelacs se détachent sur un fond sombre ponctué de blanc; ailleurs, d'étranges petits quadrupèdes aux queues nouées, des oiseaux qui se suivent pattes et becs entre-croisés, s'inscrivent dans la boucle de l'initiale. A côté de ces animaux désarticulés, d'autres gardent leurs formes pleins: chienne allaitant son petit, la queue saisie par un dragon ... La lettre historiée ... predomine; les personnages n'ont pas une valeur purement narrative ... mais ils sont liés intimement a la structure de la lettre ... Cette oeuvre capitale dans l'histoire de l'enluminure, à laquelle il foudrait consacrer une étude complète, montre comment un style encore mérovingien dans son essence meme, teinté fortement de celticisme, contient en germe des formes qui s'épanouirent à nouveau à l'époque romane.'

[7]   Henry 1967 (as n. 5 above), p. 65.

artist of the Corbie Psalter 'uses motifs of Insular decoration, chiefly interlace and animal interlace. But he involves them in compositions which are new to Insular art, some of which appear also in the Book of Kells'.[8] She reproduced several such examples from the Corbie Psalter, without detailed comment, and published her own line drawings of the letters 'In' of 'Inludebant' from Kells fol. 283r and the initial 'N' of 'Nisi' from Corbie fol. 108r to illustrate the similarities.[9] She remarked also on the use in both manuscripts of a motif derived from Byzantine manuscripts, 'the Byzantine blessing hand',[10] providing an example from the Corbie Psalter fol. 63r ('faithfully reproduced', as she said, from its model) and comparing this with the use of a similar motif in Kells fol. 58v. It should be pointed out, in passing, that in Kells fol. 58v the artist has drawn a foot rather than a hand. A similar device appears in a detail of the Book of Kells fol. 89r, where a horseman points to a passage of text with his foot.

Other similarities between the Book of Kells and the Corbie Psalter were noted in the *Proceedings* of the 1992 conference on the Book of Kells. Christian de Mérindol used the occurrence of the motif of mutual beard-pulling which appears in several pages of the Book of Kells (notably in an initial on fol. 253v) and in the Corbie Psalter fol. 73r as the starting point of a study of the diffusion of the motif up to the Romanesque period.[11] Peter Harbison noted a similarity between the initial 'M' of the *Magnificat* in the Corbie Psalter fol. 136v and the initial of the same word in Kells fol. 191v.[12] Here, however, the similarity is apparent only in the general shape of the

[8] Henry 1974 (as n. 5 above), p. 215. Henry was cautious about the possible influence of Carolingian on Insular art, a question also left open by J. J. G. Alexander, *Insular Manuscripts, 6th to the 9th Century* (A Survey of Manuscripts Illuminated in the British Isles, J. J. G. Alexander [ed.], vol. 1), London 1978, p. 16. Corbie fols 22r and 56r contain examples of the initial 'I' with simple interlace and animal terminals.

[9] Henry 1974 (as n. 5 above), p. 216. Closely similar letter formations can also be seen in Kells fols 256v and 257v.

[10] See L. Brubaker, 'The Introduction of Painted Initials in Byzantium', *Scriptorium* 45, 1991, pp. 37–8.

[11] 'Du livre de Kells et du Psautier de Corbie à l'art roman: origine, diffusion et signification du thème des personnages se saisissant à la barbe', *Kells Conference Proceedings* 1994 (as n. 1 above), p. 290. Other occurrences in the Book of Kells include the top left corner-piece at fol. 27v, and top right on fol. 188r. See B. Meehan, *The Book of Kells. An Illustrated Introduction to the Manuscript in Trinity College, Dublin*, London 1994, pls. 43–4, 90, 93. Beard pulling is featured on the underside of the ring of the west side of the Market Cross at Kells itself, and at the base of the shaft on the north side of Muiredach's Cross at Monasterboice; see *Kells Conference Proceedings* 1994 (as n. 1 above), pls. 94–5.

[12] P. Harbison, 'High Crosses and the Book of Kells', *Kells Conference Proceedings* 1994 (as n. 1 above), p. 267.

letter, there being a closer resemblance between the 'M' of Kells fol. 191v (Fig. 1) and the initial 'M' of 'Misericordias' in the Corbie Psalter fol. 80r (Fig. 3).

It is possible to add substantially to these examples of decorative content and technique common to the Book of Kells and the Corbie Psalter, particularly in examining the zoomorphic formation of letters. In Corbie fol. 68v, two peacocks (so identified from their crests) form the uprights of an initial 'A', with a snake helping to form the bar of the letter, in a style little altered from its Merovingian antecedents,[13] while on other pages of the Corbie Psalter, differing combinations of animals make up the same letter. On fol. 23v, for example, the initial 'A' of the phrase 'Ad te domine clamabo' (Psalm 27.1) is composed of a peacock and a fish. This is similar in content, though not in form, to a spectacular detail of Kells fol. 253v,[14] and again seems to be a static, prosaic version of an earlier model. In Kells, broadly similar examples of the initial 'A' are frequently composed of lions, drawn with a fluidity and inventiveness not matched by the Corbie Psalter. In initial 'As' in Kells fols 116v and 273r, two elongated lions embrace or grapple. In the initial 'A' of the phrase 'Ab arbore' on fol. 105r, two lions face in the same direction as they appear to tumble over each other. On fol. 255v (line 5) a lion and a man are combined with a bird, and on fol. 269v the letter is formed ingeniously from a single lion. In Corbie fol. 86r two sets of confronted birds, less readily identifiable but probably again peacocks, form the bars of an 'E' in a manner similar to details of Kells fols 2r and 285v.[15] Other animal motifs appear in the two manuscripts. In versions of a late classical device, peacocks consume grapes from chalices in the Corbie Psalter fol. 40r, while birds which are probably to be understood as doves do likewise on fol. 55v, and again in the initial letter of 'Beatus' on fol. 95r. The same motifs run through the Book of Kells.[16] On Corbie fol. 75r, a peacock stands on a snake, an image which refers to Psalm 90.13, 'Thou shalt walk upon the asp',[17] and is reminiscent of a detail of Kells fol. 8r. In the Corbie Psalter fol. 20v (Fig. 2), four interlaced birds (doves or perhaps ducks) rotate within the bowl of the letter 'D'. This common Insular motif strongly resembles the three birds within the bowl of a 'Q' in Kells fol. 152v (Fig. 4) and in Corbie fol. 20v, another bird is pictured above the letter. Henry illustrated a similar initial 'D' from the Corbie Psalter fol. 33v.[18]

[13] See Micheli 1939 (as n. 6 above), pl. 125. N. Netzer, *Cultural Interplay in the Eighth Century. The Trier Gospels and the Making of a Scriptorium at Echternach*, Cambridge 1994, pp. 50–4 discusses the Merovingian style of initial in Insular manuscripts.

[14] Henry 1974 (as n. 5 above), pl. 123; Meehan 1994 (as n. 11 above), pl. 65.

[15] Micheli 1939 (as n. 6 above), pl. 123; Meehan 1994 (as n. 11 above), pls. 65, 71.

[16] See Meehan 1994 (as n. 11 above), pp. 57–63.

[17] Ibid., pl. 67.

[18] Henry 1974 (as n. 5 above), p. 219, fig. 71 (top right).

A form of allusive, indirect illustration is employed occasionally in the Book of Kells. On fol. 67r, for example, a cock and hens appear to illustrate the parable of the seed and the sower. In the Corbie Psalter fol. 94r, similarly, a hound suckles her young at the opening of Psalm 109, a text which contains the phrase 'ex utero ante luciferum genui te' ('from the womb before the day-star I begot thee'). An illustrative intent is more frequently clear in the decoration of Corbie than it is in Kells. In Corbie fol. 14r a figure clutches a cross in direct imitation of the grasping or consuming of the symbols of Christ which is such a dominant feature of the Gellone Sacramentary and which may be interpreted in a detail of Kells fol. 96r.[19] To take another example, on fol. 29r of the Corbie Psalter a helmeted warrior with a spear and shield points to an appropriate word in the text, 'pugna'. On fol. 81r a man blows a trumpet to signify the praise of God expressed in Psalm 95.

In the decoration of both manuscripts there is a tendency to draw attention to the mouth. The mouths of the peacock and the snake touch in Corbie fol. 75r, an image to which reference has already been made. In Kells fol. 19v (at the centre of the lower section of the 'Z' of 'Zacha / riae') a peacock bites the lower jaw of a lion. At the foot of Kells fol. 111r, a peacock's head is within the mouth of a lion, a motif which is repeated several times in the zoomorphic interlace of Kells fol. 200r. In Corbie fol. 113v, two men are depicted with their own beards in their mouths. They are similar to two men in Kells fol. 201v, and to the man biting his own hair in Kells fol. 68v. Another figure in Corbie fol. 113v (Fig. 5) has a strand of foliage in his mouth, similar to a figure in Kells fol. 53v (Fig. 6) who holds an interlacing tendril in his mouth. Tongues, drawn in more or less stylised forms, emanate from the mouths of various creatures, particularly lions, in these manuscripts. What might lie behind this device, which was common in both earlier and later periods, remains to be determined with certainty. It seems to accord with the last words of Christ's ancestor David, 'The spirit of the Lord hath spoken to me, and his word by my tongue' (II Kings 23.2), the lion, symbol of the house of Judah, representing David in this context. The tongues are frequently presented as foliage, recalling a phrase from Proverbs 15.4, 'A peaceable tongue is a tree of life'.[20]

Other instances where attention is drawn to the mouth occur more precisely at points where the text indicates it to be appropriate. In the Corbie Psalter fol. 67v there is a depiction of Mary with an angel, who holds a finger in his mouth at the phrase 'Uoce mea ad Dominum clamaui' (Psalm 76.2). In Corbie fol. 92r (Fig. 7) a man holds his finger in the mouth of a fish or

[19] Meehan 1994 (as n. 11 above), pl. 81.
[20] In an Egyptian limestone frieze of the fifth or sixth century now in the Liverpool Museum, a lion, placed within an inhabited vine-scroll, holds the vine in its mouth. See *Byzantium. Byzantine Art and Culture from British Collections*, Exh. Cat. British Museum, D. Buckton (ed.), London 1994, p. 65, no. 54.

dolphin at the phrase 'Paratum cor meum Deus paratum cor meum cantabo' (Psalm 107.2). In Corbie fol. 92v a snake and a man appear to have their tongues in each other's mouths at the phrase 'Os peccatoris' (Psalm 108.2).[21] In Corbie fol. 23v, a bird's beak is in a fish's mouth at the opening of the phrase 'Ad te Domine clamabo' (Psalm 27.2). Similar representations occur in the Book of Kells. In Kells fol. 252v (Fig. 8), line 4, for example, two lions form the first two letters of the word 'Dicebat' (Luke 16.1), both lions holding their paws to their mouths. In Kells fol. 83v, another two lions perform the same action, the words 'dixit' and 'dicit' appearing in the verses above (Matthew 18.21–22).[22] On Kells fol. 117r, a lion bites his own rear paw at the beginning of the phrase 'Tunc ait illi ihs' (Matthew 26.52). On Kells fol. 274v, a lion helping to form the word 'dico' (Luke 22.16) does the same. In Kells fol. 254r two lions compose the initial letter of the word 'omnis' (Luke 16.18). The hind paw of one is placed in the mouth of the other, whose own hind paw touches the tongue of his companion, but on this occasion no word referring directly to speech appears in the verse, which concerns adultery. In a similar example on Kells fol. 260r, a lion touches his tongue with his hind paw. The text refers, however, not to speech but to hearing, since the lion forms the first letter of the phrase 'His ille auditis' (Luke 18.23). Such an example serves to demonstrate a certain indifference on the part of the artists of the Book of Kells towards connecting text and image directly.

One palaeographical feature common to the two manuscripts may be noted. In several pages of the Book of Kells, elements of the decoration were in place before the completion of the script.[23] The same practice occurs in the Corbie Psalter, on fols 7r and 25r, as Ganz has observed, and perhaps in addition on fol. 81r.[24]

Further parallels between aspects of the decoration of the Corbie Psalter and the Book of Kells may assist in the understanding of certain stylistic and iconographic features of the Book of Kells which have not to date attracted detailed comment. The decoration of fol. 188r (Figs 9–10) has posed particular problems of interpretation. On this page, human figures are engaged in a

[21] Reproduced in *Kells Conference Proceedings* 1994 (as n. 1 above), pl. 112. A number of later parallels can be found, in, for example, a late twelfth-century English chess piece (a rook) in the British Museum (M&LA 81, 3–8, 1. BM Ivories 33) in which two beasts (lions?) embrace, their tongues in each other's mouths. J. Williams, *The Illustrated Beatus. A Corpus of the Illustrations of the Commentary on the Apocalypse*, 5 vols, London 1994, vol. 1, p. 151, pl. 94 shows a peacock with its beak in a fish's mouth, forming the letter 'D', in a tenth-century Biblia Hispalense (Madrid, Bibl. nacionale, MS Vit. 13–1, fol. 201v).

[22] Reproduced in *Kells Conference Proceedings* 1994 (as n. 1 above), pl. 24.

[23] *The Book of Kells, MS 58, Trinity College Library Dublin: Commentary*, P. Fox (ed.), Lucerne 1990, p. 255.

[24] Ganz 1990 (as n. 1 above), p. 133. The rubrics were generally written after the decoration of the page, to judge from those on fols. 77v, 79r, 106v and 133r.

variety of activities among the last four letters of the word 'Quoniam', at the opening of Luke's Gospel. Not all of these activities are readily explained in terms of Christian iconography, nor do they accord in an entirely satisfactory way with themes suggested for the the page as a whole.[25] Françoise Henry felt that the page contains an indirect depiction of the Harrowing of Hell or the Descent into Limbo, a scene 'frequently represented in Byzantine painting, though in a much more matter-of-fact way'.[26] George Henderson agreed substantially with this interpretation, while remarking on the general resemblance of the figure style to that of the eighth-century Franks casket.[27] A scene of the entry of the damned into the jaws of hell in a late eighth- or early ninth-century ivory carving of the Last Judgement (Victoria and Albert Museum, inv. 253:1867) may be compared directly with the detail in Kells fol. 188r of two figures whose heads are held within the mouths of lions. The parallel even extends to the resemblance between the crescent border which encloses the damned in the ivory and the shape of the 'a' of 'Quoniam' in the manuscript. Françoise Henry regarded the Victoria and Albert ivory, incidentally, as having several features in common with manuscripts from the Amiens region.[28] Similar, though later, depictions of the damned entering the mouth of hell appear on the twelfth-century carved tympanum of the church of Sainte-Foy at Conques, and in a thirteenth-century stained-glass window at Saint-Étienne, Bourges.[29] At the top of fol. 188r, the open mouth of a lion looms above another member of the damned, a headless one, as the figure itself was left undrawn by the artist. The act is observed by an audience of two figures who lie sideways in the panel below. Further confirmation that the scene in Kells fol. 188r depicts the Descent into Hell is provided by an image in the Corbie Psalter fol. 110r (Fig. 11) of a figure held by the ankles being lowered head first into the mouth of a beast. Clearly the image is intended to represent hell, since it accompanies the text of Psalm 129 which begins 'De profundis clamavi'.[30] It resembles those heads within the letter 'N' of Kells fol. 188r which hang down in a manner that is so contorted as to indicate that the whole figure is inverted. A similar device occurs in the lower right corner-piece of the Book of Kells fol. 27v, where the necks of the four figures are greatly elongated in order to accommodate the unnatural position

[25] Meehan 1994 (as n. 11 above), pp. 71–2.
[26] Henry 1974 (as n. 5 above), pp. 203–4.
[27] G. Henderson, *From Durrow to Kells. The Insular Gospel-books 650–800*, London 1987, pp. 165–8.
[28] Henry 1967 (as n. 5 above), p. 169.
[29] J. R. Benton, *The Medieval Menagerie. Animals in the Art of the Middle Ages*, New York 1992, pp. 60–1.
[30] There may be resonances of Jonah and the whale in this image, as suggested by Kuder 1977 (as n. 1 above), p. 114, and thus of Christ's death and resurrection. See J. O'Reilly in *Kells Conference Proceedings* 1994 (as n. 1 above), p. 354.

of their heads. On fol. 188r, a further figure is placed upside down in a ten-figure panel at the top of the page. The disposition of these figures in the Book of Kells seems to provide an oblique allusion to the theme of the Descent into Hell, in contrast to the explicit rendering of the Corbie Psalter and other sources. The five figures whose heads and shoulders appear above the letters 'am' refer to the theme of the Last Judgement, being strongly reminiscent of the twelve Apostles, arrayed in two lines of six, in the Last Judgement scene of St Gall MS 51, p. 267.[31] The outer left figure is missing from the version in Kells fol. 188r, as its place is occupied by the top of the letter 'I'.[32]

The Corbie Psalter may again assist in the interpretation of a detail of the Book of Kells fol. 124r (Fig. 12), a page which reads TUNC CRU / CIFIXERANT XPI CUM / EO DU / OS LA / TRONES (Matthew 27.38). The significance of this passage is reinforced by its decoration. The last five words form a cross, while three inset panels contain groups of five profile figures (Fig. 13), each group arranged in a cruciform formation, looking across to the page opposite, fol. 123v.[33] This page is blank (apart from modern scribbles) but originally it was intended that it should contain a depiction of the Crucifixion.[34] A disc is placed between the heads of the upper pairs of figures in each panel, a puzzling device for which no published explanation has been offered. The discs in the lower two panels are red, while the top disc is smaller and light brown in colour, with a black dot at its centre. Similar discs are placed on the tunics of several of the figures. Though they lack a pin, they presumably represent brooches, being similar to those worn by figures in the bottom panel of the east face of the broken cross at Kells (Co. Meath), where the Baptism of Christ is represented.[35] The cross at Moone (Co. Kildare) provides

---

[31]   Alexander 1978 (as n. 8 above), pl. 206.

[32]   There is a resemblance also to the single line of Apostles in an Ascension scene on a ninth- or tenth-century Palestinian silver dish now in the Hermitage Museum, St Petersburg; see Harbison 1992 (as n. 1 above) vol. 3, fig. 891.

[33]   For a discussion of fol. 124r see J. O'Reilly, 'Early Medieval Text and Image: the Wounded and Elevated Christ', *Peritia* 6–7, 1987–88, pp. 99–100. The form of the heads bears a striking resemblance to the profile of a South Arabian bearded head in alabaster from the first century BC/AD sold at Sotheby's, 7–8 July 1994. A photograph of the head is reproduced from the auction catalogue in *Minerva. The International Review of Ancient Art and Archaeology* 5, September–October 1994, p. 32, fig. 18.

[34]   See Meehan in *The Book of Kells* 1990 (as n. 23 above), p. 247.

[35]   See Harbison 1992 (as n. 1 above), vol. 2, fig. 326; Henry 1967 (as n. 5 above), pl. 97, lower. Pinned brooches appear on a carving of a caryatid in White Island (Co. Fermanagh), Henry 1967 (as n. 5 above), pl. I. Another parallel, though an inexact one, is in the same panel of the broken cross at Kells, where two circles represent the sources of the Jor and the Dan, see Harbison 1992 (as n. 1 above), vol. 1, p. 101.

an equally strong parallel to the five heads as well as to the discs placed between the men's heads. At the base of the south side of that cross is a carving of the Multiplication of the Loaves and Fishes, in which the loaves are represented as five round objects arranged in a cruciform configuration.[36] The image may carry resonance of Jesus's declaration that he was the bread of life (John 6.35).

More precise parallels to the device between the heads of the figures appear in the Corbie Psalter. Firstly, in Corbie fol. 73r (Fig. 14), two men crouch inside the bowl of a 'Q' at the opening to Psalm 79, each pulling the other's beard, a stylised gesture that may relate to verse 7, 'inimici nostri subsannaverunt nos' ('our enemies have scoffed at us'). Between their heads is a circle which forms a detail of the internal decoration of the outline of the letter, resembling in this respect the Virgin's halo in Kells fol. 7v or St John's halo in fol. 291v, a device borrowed from Byzantine models.[37] Another close parallel to the discs of Kells fol. 124r appears in an illustrative feature of the Corbie Psalter fol. 123v (Fig. 15), where a stone slung by David at Goliath has landed high on the giant's head.[38] The larger discs of Kells fol. 124r resemble David's stone in shape and scale. David's encounter with Goliath is known from other Insular sources. It appears on several of the Irish high crosses, and in a tenth-century psalter (London, British Lib. MS Cotton Vitellius, F. xi, fol. 1r).[39] As a relatively common theme, it may well have been familiar to the artists of the Book of Kells.

What additional themes might the discs in Kells fol. 124r, or the circle between the heads of the beard-pullers in Corbie fol. 73r, have brought to mind in an audience familiar with a broad range of Christian symbolism? It may be suggested that these devices refer symbolically to the early and widespread image of Christ represented as the Lamb of God in conjunction with a cross. This theme appears on fol. 2v of the Corbie Psalter, where the Lamb of God is borne by an angel, an image derived ultimately from the pagan theme of Victory holding a wreath, and so suggesting the victory of Christ over death.[40] While Roger Stalley has pointed out that the Lamb of

[36] Harbison 1992 (as n. 1 above), vol. 1, p. 155; vol. 2, fig. 513.

[37] See for example the mosaic of the Emperor Justinian in Sant'Apollinare Nuovo, Ravenna, reproduced in O. von Simson, *Sacred Fortress. Byzantine Art and Statecraft in Ravenna*, Princeton 1987, frontispiece. Other examples in the Book of Kells of discs joined to form a circle include fol. 178v (lower left), where the body of a contorted peacock is similarly decorated, and fol. 263v, an example damaged by abrasion. In several other pages, such as fol. 188r, single circles mark the junctions between the letters. These may have been intended to replicate the nails attaching the metalwork decoration of a shrine to its internal box.

[38] The image is reproduced in colour in *Les Manuscripts de l'abbaye de Corbie. Exposition du 10 au 16 novembre 1991*, C de Mérindol and G. Garrigou (eds), Corbie 1991, p. 17.

[39] Harbison 1992 (as n. 1 above), vol. 1, pp. 217-9; vol. 2, figs. 735-8.

God is carved within a roundel on the west face of the cross of Sts Patrick and Columba at Kells (Co. Meath) but is absent from the Book of Kells itself,[41] it may be that this theme is represented, although indirectly, on fol. 124r, the cross being formed by the group of five heads and the Lamb being suggested by the discs.[42] This interpretation is supported by comparison with a sixth-century mosaic in the sanctuary of the church of Sant'Apollinare in Classe, Ravenna where a scene of the Transfiguration is merged with an image of the cross at the centre of an enormous roundel. The face of Christ, itself surrounded by a halo composed of circles, is at the centre of the cross, while lambs form a dominant feature of the surrounding scene.[43] The figure of Christ within a roundel or halo was a common device in Byzantine icons, inspired by the style of late Roman portraiture such as was employed in metalwork and consular diptychs.[44] In a seventh-century icon of Sts Sergius and Bacchus from the monastery of St Catherine on Mt Sinai, for example, Christ's face appears as a small roundel between the nimbed heads of the two saints, strongly recalling the image in Kells fol. 124r.[45] Similarly, fourth-century Roman bowls show Sts Peter and Paul flanking the christogram inscribed within a circle.[46] A manuscript like the Book of Kells drew on a system of symbolism so long established and so clearly understood that elements from it could be used in an allusive manner. In other words, the conjunction of lamb, circle and cross was so commonly seen and accepted as a symbol of Christ that in Kells fol. 124r a solidly-coloured disc could function

[40] See *Age of Spirituality. Late Antique and Early Christian Art, Third to Seventh Century,* Exh. Cat. Metropolitan Museum of Art, K. Weitzmann (ed.), New York 1979, pp. 535–6. A mosaic resembling this is in the apsidal arch of San Vitale, Ravenna: see von Simson 1987 (as n. 37 above), pl. 31. On the Byzantine Pola casket, two lambs flank a wreath which surrounds a cross, see *Age of Spirituality* 1979, p. 595, fig. 83.

[41] *Kells Conference Proceedings* 1994 (as n. 1 above) p. 260; Harbison 1992 (as n. 1 above) vol. 3, fig. 943. A similar figure is on the east face of the Durrow cross; see Harbison 1992 (as n. 1 above), vol. 3, fig. 939.

[42] The Book of Kells contains many examples of animals depicted within roundels or otherwise confined within strictly defined shapes, see, for example, a snake on fol. 54v, peacocks on fol. 66v, a contorted man on fol. 67r, a lion on fol. 225v, a bird on fol. 234v, and the evangelist symbols on fol. 129v. See also Henry 1967 (as n. 5 above), pp. 165–7.

[43] Von Simson 1987 (as n. 37 above), pp. 41–3, pls. 21–3.

[44] For examples, see *Age of Spirituality* 1979 (as n. 40 above), pp. 49, 53, 97–9, 304, 308, 319.

[45] Ibid., p. 548. I am grateful to Dr Anna Contadini for drawing my attention to this icon. In an icon of St Peter from the same period and monastery, Christ's head and shoulders are placed in a roundel above the head of the Apostle, and are flanked by roundels containing the Virgin and St John the Evangelist: see *Age of Spirituality* 1979 (as n. 40 above), pp. 543–4.

[46] Ibid., pp. 569–71.

as a further reminder of the cross and therefore of Christ's Passion and triumph over death. Similar allusions to the central preoccupation of the cross may be embedded elsewhere in the decoration of the Book of Kells. The discs in fol. 124r are strikingly similar to the red disc to the left of the temple on the Temptation page of the Book of Kells fol. 202v, and also to the shields of the spearsmen on fol. 4r, top left and right, where an allusion seems to be made to the Crucifixion, a reference again to the theme of fol. 124r.[47]

The decoration of the Book of Kells has not as yet been subjected to the detailed description and analysis which is necessary to understand fully the intentions of its artists. Comparisons with the Corbie Psalter are instructive, as the Amiens manuscript seems to present certain decorative elements and illustrative themes in a manner which is clear and unambiguous, whereas the decoration of the Book of Kells frequently takes a more cryptic form. It is clear that a motif or illustration used at one place and time could be copied, adapted or transformed to suit a different context. As Porcher demonstrated, Carolingian artists in Reims were capable of borrowing themes from the *Physiologus* and placing them out of their original context in other works.[48] In the case of the Book of Kells, incongruities in the decoration such as, for example, the interlinear wolf on fol. 76v, may perhaps be explained as borrowings from inappropriate sources. Yet it seems likely that further unexplained aspects of the decoration of the Book of Kells might be elucidated through a fuller study of contemporary continental manuscripts.[49] One example of such an incongruity occurs on fol. 187v, at the conclusion of St Mark's Gospel. The text is arranged within the upper and lower triangles formed by a St Andrew's cross. On the right side of the cross is a winged lion, while on the left side of the cross is a winged human figure holding a book. This figure is identified in red ink on fol. 187v as 'angelus domini'. Despite the identification, the figure has generally been regarded as a depiction of the man, symbol of St Matthew, in conjunction with the lion, symbol of St Mark.[50] Françoise Henry made the additional suggestion that the original

[47] The disc also resembles the millstone held by an angel in the Bamberg Apocalypse of *c.*1007 (Bamberg, Stadtsbibl. MS bibl. 140, fol. 46r), reproduced in P. D'Ancona and E. Aeschlimann, *The Art of Illumination*, London 1969, pl. 45. The discs between the heads of the figures on Kells fol. 124r differ from the eucharistic devices shown on other pages of the manuscript, such as the red disc, marked into quarters, which is in the mouth of the lion on fol. 29r, see Meehan 1994 (as n. 11 above), p. 44. I owe a great deal regarding the above comments on Kells fol. 124r to discussions with Felicity O'Mahony.

[48] J. Porcher, 'Book Painting' in *Carolingian Art*, J. Hubert, J. Porcher and W. F. Volbach (eds), London 1970, pp. 112–3.

[49] Peter Harbison has employed telling comparisons with Carolingian artefacts and manuscripts in, 'Three Miniatures in the Book of Kells', *Proceedings of the Royal Irish Academy* 58, 1985, pp. 181–94.

[50] See *Kells Conference Proceedings* 1994 (as n. 1 above), p. 278; Meehan 1994 (as n. 11

intention of the artist may have been that the page should carry an image of the Ascension, the subject of the text on fol. 187v, 'such as is found in the Turin gospels, where the *angelus Domini* would have his normal place and that this scheme was forestalled by an unforeseen overflow of the text'.[51] A different iconographic intention behind the figure in Kells fol. 187v is suggested by an image in the Harley Golden Gospels (London, British Lib. MS Harley 2788), a Carolingian gospel book made probably in the eighth century.[52] Fol. 109r of the Harley manuscript carries the opening words of St Luke's gospel. The bowl of the 'Q' of 'Quoniam' takes the form of a large roundel, enclosing a depiction of the 'angelus domini' appearing to 'Zacharias', both figures identified thus. On either side of the main roundel are the heads and shoulders of 'Elizabeth' and 'Maria'. The image is clearly an illustration of an episode at the opening of St Luke's Gospel (1.5-20), Zachariah's vision of the angel Gabriel and the angel's announcement of the impending birth of St John the Baptist. The 'angelus domini' of Kells fol. 187v, which faced an opening of St Luke's Gospel on fol. 188r, may perhaps be understood in this context, as referring to an episode which was to be described close to the opening of Luke. That few depictions of the scene seem to have survived from the period[53] serves to illustrate the range and variety of the models available to the artists of the Book of Kells and to indicate the extent of the losses suffered by the great Irish monastic libraries.[54]

*This article, 'with all faults' (as book dealers put it), appeared first in *A Miracle of Learning. Studies in Manuscripts and Irish Learning. Essays in Honour of William O'Sullivan*, T. Bernard, D. Ó Cróinín, and K. Sims (eds), London 1998, pp. 29–39. It appears here, with some minor changes, by kind permission of the editors.

above), pp. 22-3.

[51] Henry 1974 (as n. 5 above), p. 173.

[52] *Codices Latini Antiquiores*, E. A. Lowe (ed.) Pt. II. Great Britain and Ireland, Oxford 1935, p. 22, no. 198; D. A. Bullough, 'Roman Books and Carolingian *renovatio*', *Studies in Church History* 14, 1977, pp. 37-40.

[53] The late tenth-century Boulogne Gospels (Boulogne, Bibl. municipale MS 11, fol. 62r is the only example listed in *Insular and Anglo-Saxon Illuminated Manuscripts. An Iconographic Catalogue c. A.D. 625 to 1100*, T. H. Ohlgren (ed.), New York 1986, p. 110.

[54] I regret that this article was already written when John Higgitt reminded me of his reference to Harley 2788 in his review, 'A Strictly Limited Edition: the New Facsimile of the Book of Kells', *Art History* 14, 1991, p. 450.

Eloquent Ornament: Exegesis and Entanglement in the Corbie Psalter

HEATHER PULLIAM

The Corbie Psalter reveals its mixed artistic heritage in its combination of Carolingian and Insular styles and in its inclusion of Byzantine and Merovingian motifs.[1] Many early Carolingian manuscripts contain both Insular and Carolingian elements, but the decorated initials of the Corbie Psalter form a uniquely seamless hybrid between the two styles. Many of its initials contain human figures and may be classified as historiated, making clear reference to events prophesied or described in the Psalms and their commentaries.[2] Others consist of the knotted human figures and serpents, the heads of birds and beasts and the interlace that decorate Merovingian, Carolingian, Insular and Byzantine manuscripts, and these initials perform no other function than to adorn the text.[3]

The Corbie Psalter adapts this ornamental vocabulary introducing new levels of meaning not only to the text but also to its figurative imagery as exemplified by the Beatus initial (Fig. 1). Employing the frame of the letter, the artist presents the reader with a double image, separated and yet linked by the symmetrical form of the letter itself. David in the upper half of the initial exudes the confidence of youth and royal authority, beardless, sitting on a throne and wearing a royal purple robe. His features and pose are calm and reflective. In the initial's lower register, the artist depicts a bearded David, his

[1]   See Bernard Meehan's article in this volume for a discussion of the manuscript's place of origin.

[2]   J. Porcher first indicated the relationship between the initials and Psalm commentary in, J. Hubert, J. Porcher and W. F. Volbach, *Europe in the Dark Ages*, London 1969, p. 195.

[3]   Two notable exceptions are the Book of Kells and the Gellone Sacramentary. For discussion of the role performed by initials in these books see B. Teyssèdre, *Le Sacramentaire de Gellone et la figure humaine dans les manuscrits francs du VIIIe siècle*, n.p. 1959; F. Henry, *The Book of Kells*, London 1974, p. 215; H. Pulliam, 'Opening the Senses: The Gospel Book as an Instrument of Salvation as Articulated by the Minor Decoration and Full-Page Illustrations in the Book of Kells', PhD diss., University of St. Andrews 1998; B. Meehan, *The Book of Kells*, London 1994, pp. 68–77.

24

legs bent between kneeling and standing. His left arm reaches up in supplication to the angel floating above him.

Jean Desobry interprets the upper level of the initial as a depiction of David as Christ, noting the figure's cross nimbus, and the lower level as David being guided by an angel, who helps him to avoid 'the counsel of the ungodly' and the 'way of the sinners' described in the psalm.[4] Desobry notes the artist's skill in employing 'the lesser detail' of the double register of the initial B to convey the two voices in the psalm, that of Christ and that of David.[5] He does not discuss the four beast-head terminals, other than to describe them as serpents.[6] Although their appearance does not differ from that in countless other beast-head initials of Insular, Merovingian and early Anglo-Saxon and Carolingian manuscripts, they do not serve the same, purely decorative function. The right foot of David/Christ in the upper register extends beyond the frame of the letter and rests on top of the beast which forms the initial. This detail of the image recalls the iconography of Christ over the Beasts, the figure's extended foot recalling the words of Psalm 109, 'Sit thou at my right hand: Until I make thy enemies your footstool'.

In the scene below, Desobry argues that David's bent legs and the movement of the folds of his clothing suggest that he is marching behind the angel who leads him to the good path.[7] David's back leg bends to a much greater degree than his leading leg, and the artist articulates the bend despite the figure's flowing robes. David's back foot is clearly wedged behind the beast-head of the initial terminus. His attitude is not of someone marching, but of a man stumbling, his foot caught by the beast-head. The Psalmist frequently refers to stumbling and being prevented from falling by the hand of God, 'For he hath delivered my soul from death ... my feet from falling' and later, 'Being pushed I was overturned that I might fall; but the Lord supported me'.[8] Both Bede and Augustine when commenting on David's sin

[4]   J. Desobry, 'Le manuscrit 18 de Bibliothèque municipal d'Amiens', in *Techniques narratives au moyen-âge*, Amiens 1974, pp. 63–117, at p. 80. The manner in which the artist depicts the dual persons of David and Christ in the single, seated figure in the upper register is worth noting. The appearance of the figure, with his cross nimbus, suggests that he represents Christ, while his actions, dipping his pen in the inkwell, indicates that David, the supposed author of the Psalms, is represented. A similar conflation of the two personalities occurs in the initial for Psalm 108 (see discussion in n. 31 below).

[5]   Desobry 1974 (as n. 4 above), pp. 104, 115, points out that the artist uses this technique again to indicate the two 'voices' in Psalms 33 and 103.

[6]   The heads do not resemble those of serpents. The duck-bill shape of the muzzle appears on several creatures which are not birds, such as the beast on fol. 52r and the serpent on fol. 139r. These creatures are fantastical beasts that make no specific reference to those of the natural world.

[7]   Desobry 1974 (as n. 4 above), p. 79.

[8]   Psalms 114.8, 'quia eripuit animan meam de morte ... pedes meos a lapsu', and

emphasize that although he was falling, he was not fallen.[9] In Psalm 24.15, the Psalmist states, 'My eyes are ever towards the Lord: for he shall pluck my feet out of the snare.' In the Corbie image, David stumbles but reaches out to the angel, who pulls David up from the snare by the rim of his halo.[10] Both the psalms and patristic commentary emphasise that man by his nature stumbles, and those who fall down and cannot rise are the wicked who trust in their own might, while the penitent and humble man relies upon God's strength when he begins to fall and thereby is saved.[11]

David's foot wedged behind the beast-head terminal also alludes to the nature of his sin as described in the scriptures. Psalm 35 refers to the 'foot of pride', but David's reputation as the penitent and humbled man and the manner in which he reaches up in supplication toward the angel undercuts this explanation of the image. Patristic commentary, however, interprets the foot as signifying love or, when the love is perverse, lust.[12] The initial perhaps intimates the particular cause of David's downfall, namely his lust for Bathsheba. Not only does the artist employ the shape of the letter to link and contrast the two voices of the psalm as suggested by Desobry, he also uses its decoration for the same end. The terminus of both registers calls attention to the feet of its figures. Christ's foot rests triumphantly upon the neck of the beast; David's catches underneath its head.

The majority of Corbie initials depict creatures entangled in their own limbs, tails and tongues. In Psalm 55, two beasts form the letter 'M', their long, thick tongues binding their forelegs together. In the psalm the narrator

---

117.13, 'impulsus eversus sum ut caderem: et Dominus suscepit me'. Patristic commentators agree as to the meaning of these verses, describing man as having a tendency to stumble or beginning to fall but being prevented from falling completely by the intervention of God. Augustine, *Enarrationes in Psalmos*, 72.8 (PL, 36, col. 919), Bede, *In Psalmorum librum exegesis* 114 (PL, 93, cols 1045D and 1050B), Cassiodorus, *Expositio in Psalterium*, 114.8 and 117.13 (PL, 70, cols 820D and 830C). The same emphasis occurs throughout the Corbie Psalter, where God and his instruments appear to guide, punish and protect man in his earthly existence. Porcher 1969 (as in n. 2, above), p. 195, cites the best example, where the sleeve of the Hand of God intervenes between David and Goliath. A similar emphasis upon God's intervention occurs throughout the Book of Kells. See Pulliam 1998 (as n. 3 above).

[9] See discussion in n. 8 above.

[10] Desobry suggests that the angel carries a pilgrim staff in his left hand, which he presents to David in order to help him along the good path, Desobry 1974 (as n. 4 above), p. 80. The rod of authority carried by Byzantine angels is the most likely explanation for the staff held by the angel in Corbie. On fol. 76v an angel uses a similar staff to push down a dragon.

[11] See n. 8 above.

[12] Augustine, *Enarrationes in Psalmos*, 9.15 (PL, 36, col. 124). Similarly, Cassiodorus writes that 'feet' intimate 'perverse desires', *Expositio in Psalterium*, 9.15 (PL, 70, col. 84C).

describes his enemies plotting against him and lying in wait but concludes that God will triumph. When viewed exclusively within the context of the psalter text, the image appears purely decorative. When placed within the context of Augustine's commentary, however, its role becomes apparent, 'But let them that shall sojourn and shall hide, carp at all words, seeking somewhere to make snares and knotty false accusations, wherein they are themselves entangled before those whom they strive to entangle: in order that they themselves be taken and perish'.[13] The motif of knotty, self-entanglement occurs elsewhere in the patristic writings as well as throughout the imagery of the early middle ages.[14] But no other Western patristic writer except Augustine discusses self-ensnarement in reference to this particular psalm. If the psalter was made in the Corbie scriptorium during the late eighth century as its script and imagery suggest, the manuscript may have been written under the abbacy of Adalhard, who was known to have greatly admired Augustine.[15] During this period the scriptorium produced an extensive, multi-volume copy of Augustine's commentary on the psalms written in the same Maurdramnus script as the Corbie Psalter.

The entanglement motif appears again in the initials of Psalms 31 and 57. In the former the Psalmist describes his agony when denying his sin, 'I was turned in anguish'. The psalm concludes by warning man not to resemble the horse and mule that must be bridled. In the upper register of the letter 'B', a beast is bound by a thick cord looping around its neck and legs (Fig. 2). The cord is fleshy, beginning at the creature's tail and disappearing into its mouth. Its head and neck twist over and under, rendering into visual terms the turning 'in anguish' described in verse four of the psalm, 'conversus in aerumna mea'. Beneath, a similarly knotted beast bares its teeth and bites into its own legs. The creature, unbridled, destroys itself in its own voraciousness.

Two knotted beasts shape the initial that begins Psalm 57. The creatures have no hind legs, their bodies terminating in a tail (Fig. 3). A tendril grows from beneath their jaws and, after a series of knots, enters the mouths of the

[13]   'Illi autem qui incolent et abscondent, aucupantur verba omnia, quaerentes alicubi laqueos et nodosas facere calumnias, quibus prius ipsi implicantur quam quos implicare contendunt; ut prius ipsi capiantur et pereant, quam alios capiant ut perdant.' Augustine, *Enarrationes in Psalmos*, 55.10 (PL, 36, col. 654).

[14]   For further discussion of images of entanglement in the Book of Kells, Corbie Psalter and Insular sculpture, see Pulliam 1998 (as n. 3 above).

[15]   Ganz, in his comprehensive analysis of the Corbie scriptorium, argues that the initials and script of the Psalter suggest a Corbie origin. By the late eighth century the library was vast, containing multiple works by commentators as diverse as Bede, Jerome, Cassiodorus, Basil and Ambrose. D. Ganz, *Corbie in the Carolingian Renaissance* (Beihefte der Francia, 20), Sigmaringen 1990, p. 133 and pp. 124–44. Porcher 1969 (as n. 2 above), p. 195, noting the influence of Greek commentary on the Psalter illustrations, suggests that the manuscript was written in Corbie, which had relatively strong connections with the Byzantine church.

beasts.[16] The psalm warns the wicked, 'For in your heart you work iniquity: your hands forge injustice in the earth ... they have spoken false things ... God shall break in pieces their teeth in their mouth: The Lord shall break the grinders of lions.' The knots that bind the creatures' legs are unusually fine and symmetrical. Typically the artist makes a clear distinction between interlace and entanglement; however, the use of the verb 'concinnant' may explain the unusually regular and delicate series of interlinked knots. Augustine, commenting on the psalm, quotes Proverbs 5.22, 'With the chains of his sins each one is bound fast', and points out that sin and its subsequent punishment is self-inflicted, forged by man's own hands.[17] Similarly, Bede refers to Isaiah 5.18 'Woe to them who draw iniquity with cords of vanity', and glosses 'concinnant' as 'contexo'; to weave, intertwine or twist together.[18] The majority of commentators identify the wicked ones described in the psalm as the Pharisees who seek to trap Christ through speaking 'false things', interpreting the broken 'grinders' of lions as a reference to the high priests who, when seeking to 'bite' Christ with their questions, fall into traps of their own making.[19]

Similar associations occur in the decorated initials of the Book of Kells.[20] On fol. 122r, two brightly colored quadrupeds dominate an otherwise unremarkable page (Fig. 4). Although more typically Insular in style, they closely resemble the Corbie initials. The tongue of the upper beast wraps around its muzzle, while that of the lower beast loops around its neck. The creatures' tails wrap around their bodies, knotting their legs together. They mark out Matthew 27.26, where the Jewish population, led on by the Pharisees, cry out for Christ's crucifixion. Cassiodorus, when commenting on Psalm 57 discussed above, cites this very event as related in John's gospel as an example of false tongues leading to the downfall and damnation of the wicked. On fol. 100v of Kells, Christ criticises the Pharisees for straining at a gnat while swallowing a camel. An entangled human figure, eating his own hair, forms the initial that begins the verse. Matthew 22.34 relates how the Pharisees upon seeing that Christ has silenced the Sadducees attempt to entrap him with leading questions. The initial that begins the verse is formed by two figures wrestling with each other, entangled in their own limbs and hair. The

[16]   The 'beards' in most reproductions appear to terminate in a circle between the creatures' jaws, but in some colour reproductions and the manuscript itself, it is obvious that these do not terminate but rather disappear into the creatures' mouths. The circles merely mark the 'junctures' of tongues and beards.

[17]   Augustine, *Enarrationes in Psalmos*, 57.3 (PL, 36, col. 674).

[18]   Bede, *In Psalmorum Librum Exegesis*, 57 (PL, 93, col. 784A).

[19]   Ibid., cols 784D–785A; Augustine, *Enarrationes in Psalmos*, 57.11 (PL, 36, cols 682–83); Cassiodorus, *Expositio in Psalterium*, 57.6 (PL, 70, col. 407B–C).

[20]   See Meehan 1994 (as n. 3 above), pp. 66–7 and Pulliam 1998 (as n. 3 above), pp. 185–211.

bearded figure struggles with his hair, which serves only to tighten the bonds ensnaring his own hands. As in the Corbie Psalter, long hair and beards convey the manner in which sin emerges from man's flawed, mortal body rather than from an outside source. If he attempts to free himself from it, he will experience pain as he tugs at his own flesh.[21]

In Psalm 9 of the Corbie Psalter, a man forms the first letter of the verse, 'I will give praise to thee, O Lord, with all my heart: I will relate all thy wonders' (Fig. 5). The content of the verse and the position of the man's hands suggest that the artist intended to represent the voice of the Psalmist; however, his lower torso knots at the waist and terminates in a tri-knot, and his long, green beard loops twice around his arms, binding them together. In the text, the Psalmist celebrates God's justice and the subsequent demise of his enemies, saying in verse 17, 'The Lord shall be known when he executeth his judgements, the sinner hath been caught in the works of his own hands'. Other verses proclaim that 'their foot hath been taken in the very snare in which they hid', 'they are caught in the counsels which they devise', and, 'in his net he will bring him down'. The description of sin and error as ropes or bonds of man's own making is prevalent in much patristic commentary, appearing in the writings of Gregory, Cassiodorus, Augustine, Bede and Columbanus. The metaphor has several scriptural sources: Proverbs 5.22, Isaiah 5.18, Psalm 139 and, most explicitly, Psalm 9.

The Stuttgart Psalter interprets the Psalm quite literally, showing Christ breaking a man's arm to illustrate 'break thou the arm of the sinner'. The Corbie Psalter conveys the more abstract concepts of the psalm in a similarly literal fashion. Like the commentary on the psalm, the psalter's imagery makes clear the fact that the damnation and downfall of the wicked is self-inflicted. In Cassiodorus' commentary on Psalm 9.16, he states that the sinner is contracted to damnation by his own works, but uses the word 'astringitur', which can also be translated as to bind, fasten or tighten. In the initial, it is the hair produced from the man's face that binds his arms and the contortions of his body that render him immobile, showing his transformation into the damned, as his body changes into a coiling serpent. Instead of feet, his lower body terminates in a knot. Cassiodorus, glosses those whose 'foot hath been taken in the very snare in which they hid', as those who are bound fast by their knotty ('nodosa') deception.[22] Similarly Bede

---

[21]   Although long beards often served as a sign of penance, many perceived long hair as a sign of superfluous thoughts and an unkept beard as evidence of punishment. Gregory's *Moralia* 2.52 (CCSL, 143, 109–10), refers to 'superfluous thoughts' and Isidore of Seville's *De ecclesiasticus officiis* 2.4 (PL, 83, cols 779C–80A), refers to tonsure as stripping off 'the crimes of the body like hairs'. See G. Constable, 'Beards in History', in Buchard de Bellevaux, *Apologia de Barbis* (Corpus Christianorum Continuatio Mediaevalis, 63), Turnholt 1962, p. 70.

[22]   'Quos capitio nodosa constringent.' Cassiodorus, *Expositio in Psalterium*, 9.15 (PL,

refers to those with their foot caught as being entangled ('irretitur') in deceit.[23] Augustine in discussing the use of the word snare, points to the pain experienced by those who attempt to free themselves from the trap of their own lust.[24] Similarly, if the man depicted in the Corbie Psalter were to struggle, he would tug at his own beard and chin.

In Psalm 72, on fol. 101r, an angel holding a whip stands over a man entangled in his own beard (Fig. 6). Desobry suggests that the angel uses the man's hair as reins, illustrating Psalm 72, verses 22–4, 'For my heart hath been inflamed, and my reins have been changed ... I am become a beast before thee ... by thy will thou hast conducted me'. The figure resembles that of Psalm 9 but with notable exceptions. He is not alone but rather held up by an angel. Nor does his body terminate in a dragon's tail. He is clothed in white rather than purple, his hair and beard are gray, not an unnaturally vibrant green. His left hand is free from entanglement. Although the manner in which he tugs on his clothing might seem to refer to verse 6, 'they are covered ('operti') with their iniquity and impiety' (at least three commentators gloss 'operti' as referring to being clothed by an outer garment), several initials in the Psalter depict angels and other sacred personages holding their clothing in a similar fashion, suggesting that this is merely a stylistic habit.[25] Even though his beard binds his right hand, the figure manages to gesture to the word 'God'. Moreover, although the angel whips him with his right hand he gestures in blessing with his left.

In the psalm, the narrator describes how he had almost fallen from faith upon seeing the prosperity of the wicked. Bede's and Augustine's distinction between falling and being fallen, forms the central argument to their discussion of this psalm.[26] Bede and Cassiodorus point out that while the contrite man suffers the scourges of God during his penance, the wicked will be scourged by their own sins for eternity.[27] In the initial, David has indeed

---

70, col. 84C).

[23] 'Irretitur in dolosa cogitatione.' Bede, *In Psalmorum Librum Exegesis*, 9, (PL, 93, col. 537C).

[24] Augustine, *Enarrationes in Psalmos* 139.9 (PL, 37, col. 1810).

[25] Ibid., 72.6 (PL, 36, col. 919). Bede, *In Psalmorum Librum Exegesis*, 72 (PL, 93, col. 870B) and the Hiberno-Latin Gloss of Codex Palatinus Latinus 68, see M. McNamara, *Glossa in Psalmos: The Hiberno-Latin Gloss on the Psalms of Codex Palatinus Latinus 68* (Studi e testi, 310), Vatican City 1986, p.150. Psalm 108.18 is one possible, scriptural source for this interpretation, as it describes the wicked man putting on cursing like a garment. The Corbie Psalter, however, depicts an upright David with nimbus in Psalm 70, David/Christ in Psalm 108, Christ in the Gloria initial on 138v and an angel in Psalm 83 holding their clothes in a similar manner.

[26] See n. 8 above.

[27] Cassiodorus, *Expositio in Psalterium*, 72.5–6 (PL, 70, col. 547C) and Bede *In Psalmorum Librum Exegesis*, 72 (PL, 93, col. 870A) and, to a lesser extent, the

stumbled, but an angel of God holds him up by the hair and scourges him. Although he is indeed caught in his sin, he points with his index finger to the source of his salvation.

Repeatedly the Psalter visually distinguishes the sinful, who entangle themselves, from the good man, who is beset by outside forces. Psalm 61 describes the manner in which the wicked persecute and curse the good man (Fig. 7). Commentators interpret this as signifying the sufferings of Christ and his Church, the head and the body.[28] The initial beginning the psalm depicts two beautifully coloured silver fish, possibly a reference to Christ and the Church. A dog leaps up, biting the fish on the left while ensnaring the one on the right with its tail. The Psalmist repeatedly associates dogs with the enemies who plot against the good man.[29] The Book of Kells contains a similar initial marking the passage in which Judas and the priests plot against Christ, depicting a knotted serpent reaching up and wrapping its tail around a fish. Elsewhere in the Corbie Psalter, the tail of a dog ensnares a bird, illustrating Psalm 123, which describes the Lord's releasing man from the grasp of the wicked 'like a sparrow out of the snare'.[30]

David as Christ is depicted at Psalm 108 (Fig. 8).[31] A serpent encircles the figure, forming the inital. The creature's tail loops once around David/Christ's legs. Desobry points out that the image illustrates verses 2, 3, and 5 of the psalm, 'For the mouth of the wicked and the mouth of the deceitful man is opened against me. They have spoken against me with deceitful tongues; and they have compassed about me with words of hatred ...

[ ] *Brevarium in Psalmos* attributed to St Jerome (PL, 26, col. 1030C).

[28] Augustine, *Enarrationes in Psalmos*, 61.2 (PL, 36, cols. 729–30). The Stuttgart Psalter depicts Christ's capture and mocking within the text of Psalm 61 on folio 73r.

[29] In Psalm 58, the Psalmist describes his enemies as hungry dogs and in Psalm 21.17 he states, 'For many dogs have encompassed me: the council of the malignant hath besieged me'. Later in the same psalm, the narrator begs God, 'Deliver, O God, my soul from the sword: my only one from the hand of the dog. Save me from the lion's mouth...'.

[30] Desobry 1974 (as n. 4 above), p. 93.

[31] Bede, *In Psalmorum Librum Exegesis*, 108 (PL 93, col. 1029 D). Augustine is emphatic that the Psalmist's voice must be understood as that of Christ, *Enarrationes in Psalmos*, 108.1 (PL, 37, col. 1431). The Stuttgart Psalter also glosses the psalm as Christ speaking out against the Jews and Judas in particular, see fol. 126r. Whereas the figure discussed in n. 4 above looks like Christ but acts like David, the figure in Psalm 108 resembles David in his dress and plain nimbus but his actions, in blessing and opening his mouth, are more appropriate to Christ. Psalm 21 also presents David as Christ, showing a kneeling figure, gesturing in supplication towards the arms of an angel above. With the exception of his cross nimbus the figure resembles depictions of David throughout the Psalter. His facial features, hairstyle, clothing and lack of beard are identical to the figure of David depicted at Psalm 6.

and they have repaid me evil for good'.[32] Christian de Mérindol agrees with
Desobry and attempts to explain the unusual manner in which David/Christ's
mouth opens to receive the tongue of the serpent, suggesting that the
emphasis on the tongue relates to the pagan belief in the 'fecundity' of the
mouth.[33] In Augustine's commentary on the psalm, he explains that Christ
hid his true identity as the Son of God from his enemies, 'But this [his true
identity] did not appear, but, when his weakness appeared, lay hid, when the
mouth of the ungodly and deceitful opened upon him; and for that reason his
mouth was opened because his virtue was concealed.'[34] Christ allows evil to
act upon him. He makes no effort to free himself, but, instead, blesses the
serpent as it entangles him.

The subtlety and consistency of these initials demonstrate that the
vocabulary of entanglement could be manipulated to make fine distinctions as
demonstrated in Psalm 108. The Book of Kells shows a similar awareness and
variety in its use of knotted figures and creatures. Éamonn Ó Carragáin, in his
discussion of the Kells canon tables, notes that the small figure of Christ on
fol. 2v, shown stretched out between two beasts whose tongues seem to bind
his wrists, actually holds the creatures' tongues and thereby prevents them
from speaking.[35] More specifically, Christ grasps the tongues at their base,
rendering them powerless, making evident his ability to escape ensnarement
should he wish to do so. Elsewhere, on fol. 130r, a man is shown fighting a
beast. As with the canon table image, the dragon's tongue wraps around the
man. However, unlike Christ, he pulls the creature's tongue by its tip, which
serves only to tighten its grip. With his other hand he pulls at his own
knotted beard. Naked and alone, he cannot free himself without God's
intervention.

The ornament of entanglement in the Corbie Psalter is meaningful,
commenting upon and embroidering the content of the psalms and frequently
clarifying the identity of the figures in its decorated initials. The sinful man is
shown entangled in a web of his own making, while the innocent are captured
by others. The artists, like the psalms' commentators, emphasise that the good
man accepts his imprisonment just as Christ did, trusting in God's

[32] Desobry 1974 (as n. 4 above), p. 99.
[33] C. de Mérindol, 'Du Livre de Kells et du Psautier de Corbie à l'art roman: origine,
diffusion et signification du thème des personnages saisissant à la barbe', *The Book
of Kells. Proceedings of a Conference at Trinity College Dublin, 6–9 September 1992*,
F. O'Mahoney (ed.), Dublin 1994, p. 299.
[34] 'Hoc autem non apparebat, sed apparente infirmitate ejus latebat, cum os
peccatoris et os dolosi super eum apertum est; et ideo illud apertum est, quia
operta virtus hujus fuit'. Augustine, *Enarrationes in Psalmos*, 108.2 (PL, 37, col.
1432).
[35] É. Ó Carragáin, '"Traditio evangeliorum" and "sustentatio": The Relevance of
Liturgical Ceremonies to the Book of Kells', in *Kells Conference Proccedings 1994*
(as n. 33 above), p. 426.

providence, while the fallen engage in a solitary struggle which serves only to tighten the knots that bind them. Patterns of meaning, although imperceptible on a cursory examination, are evident throughout the manuscript. The consistency of the imagery, not just within the Corbie Psalter but within the Book of Kells as well, demonstrates that a language of ornament, now lost, once flourished.

Medieval Charades and the Visual Syntax of the Utrecht Psalter

WILLIAM NOEL

In his fundamental study, *The Rise of Pictorial Narrative in Twelfth-Century England*, Otto Pächt makes a distinction between the vocabulary of images on the one hand, and their grammar and syntax on the other.[1] He contrasts the syntax of images derived from classical models, such as Prudentius's *Psychomachia* with those in the Bayeux tapestry, which he sees as thoroughly medieval. The difference is not one of vocabulary; indeed, as Wormald has demonstrated, the makers of the Bayeux tapestry borrowed at least one iconographic motif from the *Psychomachia* cycle.[2] Rather, the difference lies in how the picture cycles are put together in relation to the events that they portray. Pächt sums up: 'Whereas in classical narration, and in the narrative styles dependent on it, the events have to speak for themselves, here in the Bayeux tapestry we are taken on a conducted tour through history. The event and its interpretation are being presented simultaneously, often in open violation of the logic of natural illusion'.[3] Pächt was discussing styles of narrative imagery. The purpose of this paper is to explore the visual syntax of images without narrative, particularly those in the Utrecht Psalter, generally supposed to have been written at the monastery of Hautvilliers, near Rheims, in c.830.[4] I will make the case that the visual syntax of the images in the Utrecht Psalter is of a fundamentally different type to that employed in

[1] O. Pächt, *The Rise of Pictorial Narrative in Twelfth-Century England*, Oxford 1962, pp. 9–10.

[2] F. Wormald, 'The Bayeux Tapestry: Style and Design', in *F. Wormald, Collected Writings 1: Studies in Medieval Art from the Sixth to the Twelfth Centuries*, J. J. G. Alexander, T. Brown and J. Gibbs (eds), London 1984, p. 147.

[3] Pächt 1962 (as n. 1 above), p. 10.

[4] Utrecht, Universiteits Bibl. MS 32, published in facsimile as *Utrecht Psalter. Vollständige Faksimile-Ausgabe im Originalformat der Handschrift 32 aus dem Besitz der Bibliothek der Rijksuniversiteit Utrecht* (Codices selecti, 75), K. van der Horst and J. H. A. Engelbregt (eds), Graz 1984. The bibliography is vast. See most recently *The Utrecht Psalter in Medieval Art: Picturing the Psalms of David*, K. van der Horst, W. Noel and W. C. M. Wüstefeld (eds), MS't Goy and London 1996, *passim*.

narrative illustration, and that the images that result are, in a conceptual sense, the ancestors of many of the marginal fancies that abound in illustrated manuscripts in Northern Europe in the thirteenth and fourteenth centuries.

By the term 'visual syntax' I mean the way in which the elements of any given illustration are structured and arranged in relation to the text upon which they are based. Two very different examples from the Walters Art Gallery, Baltimore, help to elucidate the term. The first is a *bas-de-page* scene from Walters MS W.88, a book of Hours from French Flanders of *c*.1300–10 (Fig. 1).[5] A figure raises a jug to his lips below verse 10 of Psalm 39, 'I have declared thy justice in a great church, lo, I will not restrain my lips: Oh Lord, thou knowest it'. The figure can be related to the text 'I will not restrain my lips', for clearly this figure is not. However, the sense of the verse suggests that the figure should be declaring the justice of the Lord, and not drinking. The artist has applied an image to a small part of the verse considered as a whole. The second image is an historiated initial 'D' depicting the Annunciation at the opening of the Hours of the Virgin in Walters MS W.82, a Psalter-Hours from Ghent, of *c*.1315–25 (Fig. 2).[6] Both images illustrate texts, but their relationships to their texts are very different. The first illustrates a phrase taken from the adjacent text, while the second illustrates an event recounted in the Gospel of St. Luke 1.26–38, but with a rich pictorial tradition of its own, and only partially cited in matins of the Hours of the Virgin. The first would usually be called a literal illustration, and the second a depiction of an episode in a narrative. The pictures, of themselves, give no clue as to how they are treating the texts upon which they are based, and herein lies a potential source of confusion. It is, of course, crucial to be able to deduce the syntactical level on which any given image is operating, and this requires knowledge of the texts to which it is alluding. The Annunciation could illustrate a different text and have a completely different visual syntax; one could, for example, interpret the scene as illustrating the words 'prayer' and 'wing', from a hypothetical text such as 'flying on a wing and a prayer'.

This might appear perverse: the Annunciation is obviously an illustration of an event. Indeed, my fanciful interpretation of it as an illustration of 'a wing and a prayer' only works because a viewer can identify it as an Annunciation; if the scene depicted was not recognizable the viewer would not know that the female figure without wings was supposed to be praying. However, finally to get to my subject, the Utrecht Psalter behaves in a manner just as perverse as this example. It contains images that look as if they are illustrations of events, but actually they are illustrations of individual words. For instance, the artist of Psalm 13 in the Utrecht Psalter has certainly illustrated the word 'adders' from part of verse 3: 'The poison of adders is

5   L. M. C. Randall, *Medieval and Renaissance Manuscripts in the Walters Art Gallery, Vol. III : Belgium*, Baltimore 1997, Part 1, pp. 67–72, no. 222.
6   Ibid., pp. 77–85, no. 225.

under their lips', but in doing so he has depicted them in relation to the fool enthroned in the *tempietto* in such a way as to suggest that the adders are part of a narrative taking place at a given place and in a given moment.

This conceit in the Utrecht Psalter is quite deliberate, and extends not just locally but throughout entire illustrations. For example, there is usually no textual reference to the elaborate landscaped settings of nearly all the images in the Utrecht Psalter. They are there to give the impression that the images are related to each other in time and space, an impression that is often entirely spurious. This impression is reinforced when the artists of the Psalter rely on pictorial formulae adapted from other, often narrative, texts to illustrate the psalms. An example is the illustration of Psalm 15. 9–10: 'My flesh also shall rest in hope. Thou wilt not leave my soul in hell: nor wilt thou give thy holy one to see corruption'. On fol. 8r the artist has depicted the *Anastasis* to illustrate 'Thou wilt not leave my soul in hell', and the historical scene of the three holy women at the sepulchre to illustrate 'nor wilt thou give thy holy one to see corruption'. However, because he illustrated 'My flesh also shall rest in hope' the body is nonetheless present in the sepulchre. The presence of the body is, of course, narrative nonsense, but this is not a series of historical scenes and should not be read according to narrative principles despite initial appearances.[7]

In the illustration to the Canticle of Habbakuk on fol. 85v of the Utrecht Psalter there is an Annunciation, together with other events of Christ's life (Fig. 3). These pictures were pulled together to illustrate just half a verse. The Annunciation is not here being used as a formula to illustrate the phrase 'flying on a wing and a prayer', but it is being used as part of a formula to illustrate verse 13: 'Thou wentest forth for the salvation of the people; for salvation with thy Christ.' The image only works because it is an Annunciation, but it is not the story of the Annunciation that is being illustrated. It is, quite simply, a phrase in verse 13. The Annunciation in the Utrecht Canticle of Habbakuk is no more (and no less) the Annunciation to the Virgin than the image in the centre of the illustration to Psalm 108, on fol. 64r, is of a tree upon which someone has left behind their belongings after a picnic, as might first appear if read according to narrative principles (Fig. 4). In Psalm 108 the tree is not mentioned at all: it is merely a support on which to hang images of the words 'water', 'oil', 'garment', and 'girdle' mentioned in verses 18 and 19 of the psalm; '...like water into his entrails, and like oil in his bones. May it be unto him like a garment which covereth him; and like a girdle with which he is girded continually.' Although scholars have frequently searched the imagery of the Utrecht Psalter for history and allegory, I would argue that the use of the Annunciation in the Canticle of Habbakuk is less an

---

[7]   See K. van der Horst, 'The Utrecht Psalter: Picturing the Psalms of David', in *Utrecht Psalter* 1996 (as n. 4 above), p. 68.

interesting allegorical interpretation of the Psalm text, than an uncharacteristic failure by the artists of the Utrecht Psalter to come up with anything more than a conventional pictorial formula, a formula reliant on our knowledge of another text, to illustrate a phrase. Perhaps other allegorical scenes may be seen in the same light. Nonetheless, the special characteristic of the Utrecht Psalter is not the pictorial vocabulary by which the text is illustrated, but rather the visual syntax used to illustrate the text. A characteristic shared by all the images in the Utrecht Psalter, except one,[8] is that they all illustrate units of text of varying length (words, phrases, and even verses), combined to give the impression that they illustrate something else entirely.

Several terms have been coined to characterise the system of illustration employed in the Utrecht Psalter and its relatives. It is most usually termed 'literal illustration'. This gives the impression that the artists of the Utrecht Psalter are following the text particularly closely. This they certainly do, but artists who depict allegory and historical narrative also illustrate texts closely; this is not a feature unique to the Utrecht Psalter. Moreover, use of the term 'literal illustration' tends to give the impression that the artists of the Utrecht Psalter bring out the literal sense of the words of the text. This is not the case. The illustration of Psalm 108.18–19, discussed above, does not bring out the literal sense of the verses even though it closely illustrates the words. In more recent years the term *imagines verborum* has been coined to characterise the type of illustration employed in the Utrecht Psalter.[9] Preferable to 'literal illustration' as a term though it is, one cannot escape the fact that historical and allegorical scenes also illustrate words.

There is a parallel between the visual syntax employed by the artists of the Utrecht Psalter and the modern game of charades. In charades actors mime phrases, words, or even syllables of words, in order that the participants can eventually decipher a saying, or a title of a film or a book. To do so, they quite deliberately act out these units of text without reference to their context within the overall saying or title. This is somewhat similar to the way in which the artists of the Utrecht Psalter manipulate their texts. Moreover, in the Luttrell Psalter (British Lib. MS Add. 421130) made in the second quarter of the fourteenth century, as Lucy Sandler has demonstrated, artists visualise not only phrases and words, but, like those playing charades, even syllables of words quite out of their textual context.[10] I suggest that 'charade illustration' may be a better phrase than 'literal illustration' for the type of visual syntax seen in the Utrecht Psalter, and other images that work in a similar way.

[8]   Psalm 50, see below.
[9]   For example, L. F. Sandler, 'The Word in the Text and the Image in the Margin: The Case of the Luttrell Psalter', *Journal of the Walters Art Gallery* 54, 1996, pp. 87–99.
[10]   Ibid., p. 92.

It is often said that the Utrecht Psalter illustrates merely the concrete words and phrases of the psalm text. It is more complicated than that. For example, Psalm 2.9 reads 'Thou shalt rule them with a rod of iron, and shalt break them in pieces like a potter's vessel'. To depict this the artist has drawn a nimbed figure hitting a pot with a rod. If just concrete words were being illustrated, these words would be 'thou', 'rod', 'break', and 'potter's vessel'; in Latin 'virga', 'confringes', and 'vas figuli'. Of course this is totally inadequate to express the relationship between the image and the text. The artist has tied the two clauses together visually: nowhere in the text does it say that the Lord will break 'them' with a rod. But that is the sense implied by verse 9. The artist has mixed his metaphors to great effect, and managed to bring out the sense of the verse, as well as the sense of the words; here we see the Lord in the act of ruling. On top of this textual sense however, is a purely visual nonsense: there is no medieval text which alludes to the Lord breaking a pot with a rod. It is, after all, an odd act for the deity. In the hands of great artists, charade illustration may be very humorous. Later medieval artists, moreover, understood the jokes. The eleventh-century Anglo-Saxon artist of Paris, Bibl. nationale MS lat. 8824, illustrating Psalm 2.9 did not copy the Utrecht image; in fact they are very different. He did, however, copy the joke, which is exactly the same.[11]

Charade illustration is syntactically elastic. To demonstrate this elasticity, I will illustrate several of the ways in which the artists of the Utrecht Psalter illustrated the word 'like', that is 'tamquam' and 'sicut'. The key to illustrating the word 'tamquam' in medieval charades is somehow to link the subject with the thing to which it is likened. The simplest way to do this is to place them next to each other. Psalm 21.15–16 reads: 'I am poured out like (*sicut*) water; my strength has dried up like (*tamquam*) a pot.' To suppose that the artist of the corresponding illustration on fol. 12r of the Utrecht Psalter was not illustrating 'tamquam' and 'sicut', we would have to suppose that the Psalmist is holding the pot and the water vessel by chance (fig. 5). I suppose, rather, that the artist is using visual proximity to illustrate 'tamquam' and 'sicut'. This method of illustration runs counter to all principles of narrative illustration, in which scenes represent larger verbal units and depict events occuring through time. If we understand this as an event, in which the Psalmist is doing these things, as we do in narrative conventions, then the Psalmist looks as if he is asking for more water to fill up his bath. Again, as in Psalm 2.9, it seems that the artists are enjoying creating purely visual 'nonsense', to set alongside the verbal 'sense'. This is at least curious, if not humorous.

[11] Published in reduced facsimile, *The Paris Psalter, Ms. Bibliothèque Nationale, Fonds Latin 8824* (Early English Manuscripts in Facsimile, 18), B. Colgrave (ed.), Copenhagen 1958. The illustration is on fol. 2r.

The illustration of 'like' by visual proximity does not bring out the nature of the connection between the two parts of the metaphor. Another way to illustrate 'like' is to apply one verb to both nouns. Psalm 1.4 reads: 'not so the impious, not so, but like (*tamquam*) dust that the wind blows from the face of the earth'. In the Utrecht illustration, on fol. 1v, the artist illustrates the metaphor, which of course includes the word 'tamquam', by showing what the text actually never states; that the impious, like the dust, will both be blown from the face of the earth. The visual 'nonsense', if we read this image according to narrative conventions, is that there are some people in a sandstorm.

A third way to illustrate 'like' is to concentrate on the visual characteristics of the objects in a metaphor, i.e. to emphasize that one is like the other, not by virtue of what happens to them, but by virtue of what they look like. As van der Horst has noted, on fol. 59v of Utrecht the illustration to Psalm 103.6: 'The deep like (*sicut*) a garment is the earth's clothing', shows the sea in the guise of a garment, almost like a table cloth for the earth.[12]

It should be clear by now that profoundly different pictorial conventions separate charade illustration from narrative illustration. Visual proximity normally means 'next to' in narrative illustration, either in a spatial or a temporal sense, while it often means 'like' in charade illustration. The result is that the pictures in the Utrecht Psalter usually do not convey information about the spatial and temporal relationship of objects, even when they look as if they do. Quite how profound is this difference is made clear when the two types of illustration are juxtaposed, as they occasionally are in the Eadwine Psalter, made at Christ Church, Canterbury around 1250.[13] The lower part of the illustration accompanying Psalm 5 on fol. 10r is based on the Utrecht Psalter's illustration to the Psalm, and uses the same visual syntax. Thus on the left is the Psalmist looking up and directing his prayer to the Lord, as required by verse 3, in the middle is an open sepulchre with a demon above it, because the throat of the wicked is an open sepulchre (verse 11), and on the right are the foolish being destroyed of verses 6 and 10. However, in the upper level the artist employed narrative conventions to tell the story, recounted in the prologue to the Psalm, of Sarah and Hagar, respectively the wife and concubine of Abraham. It starts on the left, with the barren Sarah grieving while Hagar sits with her child Ismael. On the right, after Divine intervention, Abraham stands between Sarah and Hagar; Sarah now sits with her child Isaac, while Hagar and Ismael are sent packing out on the right hand side of the picture. In the upper register of the illustration we see a temporal

12   Van der Horst 1996 (as n. 7 above), p. 60.
13   Cambridge, Trinity Coll. MS R.17.1, published in reduced facsimile in, *The Canterbury Psalter*, M. R. James (ed.), London 1935; see also *The Eadwine Psalter: Text, Image, and Monastic Culture in Twelfth-Century Canterbury*, M. Gibson, T. A. Heslop and R. W. Pfaff (eds), London 1992.

sequence unfolding. It might not look like it, but very different types of pictorial space are juxtaposed in these two images.

Normally it is easy to work out which type of visual syntax is employed in any given illustration, because most images are accompanied by their texts. But there are circumstances when this is not the case. When, in 1848, Charles Cahier studied one of the ivory covers on Charles the Bald's Psalter as a narrative image, portraying events relayed in large syntactical units, he should rather have been looking at it as a charade illustration, in which events were portrayed in very small syntactical units combined together to form one pictorial whole.[14] He did not know that the scene on the ivory was taken from the Utrecht Psalter's illustration to Psalm 56, and he interpreted it as episodes from the life of Julian the Apostate. There is a medieval example of the opposite taking place. The illustration to Psalm 50 in the Utrecht Psalter is the only one to tell a story over time. Taking as its text the titulus of the psalm rather than the psalm itself, it depicts the story of Nathan rebuking David with the parable of the ewe lamb as recounted in II Samuel 12. However, the artist of Paris, Bibl. nationale MS. lat. 8846, the last English manuscript that was copied from the Utrecht Psalter in around the year 1200, read the illustration to Psalm 50, like those to all the other Psalms in the manuscript as portraying small syntactical units, when actually, just this once, he should have read it as a continuous narrative.[15] Thus, at the bottom right for example, there is not the ewe lamb being taken from the poor man, but two calves on an altar, referring to verse 21.

The problem is most acute with those images that do not illustrate the texts that they accompany, and this is the case with the eleventh-century Anglo-Saxon 'Quinity' from the *Liber Vitae* of the New Minster, Winchester (London, British Lib. MS Cotton Titus D. xxvii, fol. 75v).[16] Narrative conventions of pictorial space do not apply to this image (Fig. 6). We should see it rather, according to the syntactical rules of charade illustration, just like the images in the Utrecht Psalter from which it was largely compiled. Christ is not present twice in a spatial or temporal sense, any more than he is at once both present and absent from the sepulchre in the Utrecht Psalter's

---

[14]   C. Cahier and A. Martin, *Melanges d'archéologie*, vol. 1, Paris 1848, pp. 38–42.

[15]   Illustrations in *Psautier illustré (XIIIe S.) Reproduction des 107 miniatures du manuscrit latin 8846 de la Bibliothèque nationale*, H. Omont (ed.), Paris 1906; see also N. J. Morgan, *Early Gothic Manuscripts* [I], *1190–1250* (A Survey of Manuscripts Illuminated in the British Isles, J. J. G. Alexander [ed.], vol. 4), London 1982, no. 1.

[16]   E. Temple, *Anglo-Saxon Manuscripts, 900–1066* (A Survey of Manuscripts Illuminated in the British Isles, J. J. G. Alexander [ed.], vol. 2), London 1976, no. 77; see also *Aelfwine's Prayerbook (London, British Library, Cotton Titus D.XXVI–XXVII)* (Henry Bradshaw Society, 108), B. Günzel (ed.), London 1993.

illustration of Psalm 15:[17] rather the artist is merely illustrating two of his aspects; that he was born of the Virgin Mary, and that he is at the right hand of the Father. If we regard it as the pictorial equivalent of a textual meditation on the qualities of the Trinity, then it can be read as a perfectly orthodox image. When Kantorowicz started the scholarly debate on this image, and called this image the 'Quinity', he was looking at it with narrative eyes, while he should have been seeing it outside any consistent reference to time or space.[18] Outside a Psalter context, this picture is one of the very few in which an artist borrowed not only pictorial motifs from the Utrecht Psalter, but also its system of visual syntax. Elsewhere, elements taken from Utrecht are employed to depict events, employing narrative spatial and temporal conventions. Since the Trinity cannot be depicted, even though its qualities can be illustrated, and since it lies outside space and time, this was a brilliant choice of pictorial convention on the part of the artist of the Winchester *Liber Vitae*.

The visual syntax of the Utrecht Psalter is demonstrably and qualitatively different from that employed for narrative illustration. It invites playful manipulation of textual messages by focusing on individual words and phrases, and illustrating them in a way that runs counter to their textual meaning. The images of the Utrecht Psalter, often wrongly called naive, were born of a highly sophisticated visual and literate culture that played on the differences between words and pictures. It is, moreover, not the illustrations so earnestly and laboriously copied from the Utrecht Psalter in the Eadwine Psalter that are the Utrecht Psalter's true progeny. For while the Eadwine artists borrowed heavily from the vocabulary of the Utrecht Psalter's illustrations, they show little appreciation of their syntax. The true progeny of the Utrecht Psalter are to be found in the margins of the Luttrell Psalter, and the *bas-de-page* of Walters MS W.88, with which I started this paper. For only in the late thirteenth and early fourteenth century do we see large scale adoption of charade illustration once again, and then not at the heads of texts, but in the margins, where artists employed it to subvert the text in ways that were entirely novel.

[17]   See above, p. 36.
[18]   E. H. Kantorowicz, 'The Quinity of Winchester', *Art Bulletin* 29, 1947, pp. 73–85.

A Re-examination of the Date of an Eleventh-Century Psalter from Winchester (British Library, MS Arundel 60)

PETER KIDD

British Library, MS Arundel 60 is one of the few psalters with good quality decoration to survive from the latter half of the eleventh century.[1] The main purpose of this paper is to explore the implications of a possible new dating of the psalter using the evidence of a red cross inscribed in its Easter table.[2] I am not the first person to have noticed, and to have considered the implications of the red cross in the Easter table of Arundel 60 (I am told that Christopher Hohler was bringing it to the attention of students decades ago) but it has only recently been mentioned in print for the first time, by Simon Keynes, in a footnote which I quote here:

> A table of Easter letters in Arundel 60, fol. 11v, similar in conception to the table in Vitellius E. xviii (but without the key) covers the years from 1060 onwards (to 1367). A red cross which has every appearance of being original was placed in the box representing 1073; and it would appear to follow that the manuscript was written in that year.[3]

[1] If we take the standard *Survey* volumes of Temple and Kauffmann as our guide, we find only two other psalters attributed to a date between about 1050 and 1120; see E. Temple, *Anglo-Saxon Manuscripts, 900–1066* (A Survey of Manuscripts Illuminated in the British Isles, J. J. G. Alexander [ed.], vol. 2), London 1976, and C. M. Kauffmann, *Romanesque Manuscripts, 1066–1190* (A Survey of Manuscripts Illuminated in the British Isles, J. J. G. Alexander [ed.], vol. 3), London 1975. The whole of Arundel 60 has been published in microfiche in P. Pulsiano, *Anglo-Saxon Manuscripts in Microfiche Facsimile* (Medieval and Renaissance Texts & Studies, 137), vol. 2, Binghamton 1994, with a somewhat uneven accompanying description at pp. 13–8.

[2] A version of the present paper was drafted in 1994, at which time it was read by Michelle Brown and Nicholas Orchard, to whom I am very grateful for their valuable comments and suggestions.

[3] *The Liber Vitae of the New Minster and Hyde Abbey, Winchester: British Library Stowe 944, together with leaves from British Library Cotton Vespasian A. VIII and British Library Cotton Titus D. XXVII* (Early English Manuscripts in Facsimile, 26), S. Keynes (ed.), Copenhagen 1996, p. 115 n. 47. The red cross is noted also in Pulsiano 1994 (as n. 1 above), while in the same author's article, 'The Prefatory

Since he says no more than this on the subject I hope that the more detailed analysis offered in this paper will prove of interest.

The decoration of the psalter consists of a series of drawings of the zodiac signs in the calendar (fols 2r–7v),[4] followed by a full-page *Crucifixion* miniature (fol. 12v) in the 'shadowed outline' drawing technique (Fig. 1); these are 'Anglo-Saxon' in style. In the text of the Psalms itself there is a fully-painted *Crucifixion* (fol. 52v) (Fig. 2), and fully-painted historiated and decorated initials, each within a painted frame, marking the three-fold division of the psalms at the beginning of Psalm 1 (fol. 13r),[5] Psalm 51 (fol. 53r),[6] and Psalm 101 (fol. 85r);[7] all these are in a very different 'Anglo-Norman' style.

There is liturgical, scribal, and textual evidence that the book was made at and for one of the Benedictine houses at Winchester, but there is no firm evidence for the dating of the volume. For a long time scholars favoured a date of *c*.1060 for the psalter, including the decoration in both styles,[8] but since the idea was proposed in 1954 by C. R. Dodwell, it has been widely accepted that while the writing and 'Anglo-Saxon' decoration date from *c*.1060 the Anglo-Norman decoration is a post-Conquest addition.[9] This

---

Matter of London, British Library, Cotton Vitellius E. xviii', in *Anglo-Saxon Manuscripts and their Heritage*, P. Pulsiano and E. M. Treharne (eds), Aldershot 1998, pp. 102–3, he describes the red cross, in the context of using marks in computistical tables as dating evidence, but does not suggest that it can be used in this way in Arundel 60 itself.

[4] Fol. 6v is illustrated in O. E. Saunders, *English Illumination*, Florence and Paris 1928, pl. 24.

[5] Illustrated in Kauffmann 1975 (as n. 1 above), ill. 1; and J. A. Herbert, *Schools of Illumination: Reproductions from Manuscripts in the British Museum, Part I. Hiberno-Saxon and Early English Schools A.D. 700–1100*, London 1914, pl. 16. A detail of the initial is in F. Wormald, 'Decorated Initials in English MSS. from A.D. 900 to 1100', *Archaeologia* 91, 1945, pp. 107–35, pl. Ic.

[6] Illustrated in E. M. Thompson, *English Illuminated Manuscripts*, London 1895, pl. 7; D. Talbot Rice, *English Art 871–1100* (Oxford History of English Art, 2), Oxford 1952, pl. 79b; and in colour in G. F. Warner, *Illuminated Manuscripts in the British Museum*, London 1903, pl. 11.

[7] Illustrated in Saunders 1928 (as n. 4, above), pl. 25; and British Museum, *Reproductions from Illuminated Manuscripts, Series II*, London 1910, pl. VIII.

[8] For example, Wormald thought that the Anglo-Norman initials marked a pre-Conquest appearance of this style, *c*.1060, see Wormald 1945 (as n. 5 above), p. 126 and pl. Ic.; and F. Wormald, 'The Survival of Anglo-Saxon Illumination after the Norman Conquest', *Proceedings of the British Academy* 30, 1944, pp. 127–45, reprinted in *F. Wormald, Collected Writings 1, Studies in Medieval Art from the Sixth to the Twelfth Centuries*, J. J. G. Alexander, T. J. Brown and J. Gibbs (eds), London 1984, pp. 153–68, 182–5, and pls., at pp. 157–8; and for Margaret Rickert's similar opinion, see p. 50, below.

[9] C. R. Dodwell, 'The Inhabited Scroll in British Museum MS. Arundel 60', Appendix 2 in *The Canterbury School of Illumination 1066–1200*, Cambridge 1954,

position received support and much of its current authority from the eminent authors of the two volumes of the *Survey of Manuscripts Illuminated in the British Isles* which cover the periods either side of the Norman Conquest.[10] In the volume covering the period 1066–1190, published in 1975, Kauffmann argued that the presence of a gloss in Old English suggests a pre-Conquest date, *c*.1060, for the original writing of the book,[11] but found Dodwell's argument for post-Conquest additions convincing and suggested a date of *c*.1080. The following year Temple's volume appeared, covering the preceding period, 900–1066, and she too accepted Dodwell's analysis and gave the same datings as Kauffmann.[12]

The danger of this sort of dating, based on the assumption that 'Anglo-Saxon' decoration and the use of Old English indicates a pre-Conquest date and that Norman-influenced decoration in England dates from after the Conquest, is highlighted by the case of a manuscript in the British Library, Cotton Caligula A. xv, fols 120–143, which is written predominantly in Old English and has decoration purely Anglo-Saxon in style yet is demonstrably a post-Conquest production.[13] In this case Temple was forced to admit that

---

pp. 118–9; Dodwell did not change his opinion later, see C. R. Dodwell, *The Pictorial Arts of the West 800–1200* (Pelican History of Art), New Haven and London 1993, pp. 103, 121, 357 etc., but it should be noted that, as far as I can tell, he does not ever actually give the date of the Anglo-Norman work as '*c*.1080', always using instead phrases such as 'post-Conquest' and 'last quarter of the century'.

[10] Kauffmann 1975 (as n. 1 above), pp. 53–4, no. 1; and Temple 1976 (as n. 1 above), p. 120, no. 103.

[11] At least two psalters with post-Conquest Old English glosses survive: Salisbury Cathedral, MS 150 (gloss added *c*.1100, see *The Salisbury Psalter, Edited from Salisbury Cathedral MS. 150* (Early English Text Society, 242), C. Sisam and K. Sisam (eds), London, New York and Toronto 1959), and the 'Eadwine Psalter', Cambridge, Trinity College, MS R. 17. 1 (*c*.1155–60, see *The Eadwine Psalter: Text, Image, and Monastic Culture in Twelfth-Century Canterbury*, M. Gibson, T. A. Heslop and R. W. Pfaff (eds), London and University Park, PA 1992, esp. ch. VI).

[12] Temple was apparently under no obligation to follow Kauffmann's datings for consistency from one volume of the *Survey* to the next, since she removed the query which Kauffmann had judiciously placed after his attribution to the 'New Minster(?)'. She gives no evidence for her *c*.1060 date, and offers no stylistic comparisons, except to mention that 'The representation of Christ recalls the figure of Christ in no. 77 (Titus D.XXVII) but the figure ... has become remote and hieratic'. Cotton MS. Titus D. xxvii is securely datable to before 1029, more than thirty years earlier even by her own reckoning, so the comparison is rather too general for the purposes of dating. For Titus D. xxvii, see *Ælfwine's Prayerbook (London, British Library, Cotton Titus D. XXVI–XXVII)* (Henry Bradshaw Society, 108), B. Günzel (ed.), London 1993.

[13] N. R. Ker, *Catalogue of Manuscripts Containing Anglo-Saxon*, Oxford 1957, repr. with suppl. 1977 and 1990, pp. 173–6, no. 139.

'Though the manuscript was produced after the Conquest, the illustrations are evidence of the tenacity of the Anglo-Saxon style ...';[14] it will be useful to bear this 'tenacity of the Anglo-Saxon style' in mind during the following discussion.

It is interesting in this context to note that another 'relentlessly Anglo-Saxon' illuminated psalter from Winchester (London, British Lib. MS Cotton Tiberius C. vi), which also was for a long time thought to date from c.1050,[15] has recently been shown to have a *terminus post quem* of 1064 and is quite probably another post-Conquest product.[16] It had, therefore, always been dated more than a decade too early.

Since most scholars have apparently found Dodwell's hypothesis concerning Arundel 60 convincing (in almost fifty years no one has challenged it publicly, to my knowledge, while many have accepted it) it will be necessary to review closely his argument. But before looking in detail at his analysis our scepticism should be aroused by the fact that his division into two separate decorative campaigns either side of the Conquest presents the obvious problem that if the fully-painted work is indeed twenty years later than the original writing and pen-drawn decoration of the book, then the three pages which were always intended to bear the most important textual decoration, the tri-partite division of the psalter at the start of Psalms 1, 51 and 101, would have remained blank for two decades. Several points need to be made about his remarks so I shall quote him *in extenso*. He states that:

[14]   Temple 1976 (as n. 1 above), p. 122. It is perhaps also worth noting here that the traditional *terminus post quem* of 1073 for the writing of this manuscript (see e.g. Ker 1957 etc. (as n. 13 above), pp. 175–6, is perhaps one year too late. The evidence on which the date relies is a series of annals written by the original scribe alongside a series of calendrical tables which are written across double-page openings, with the number of the year A.D. in the first column, at the extreme left of the left-hand page, and the annal added in the last column, at the extreme right of the right-hand page. For an illustration of a double-page spread, see G. N. Garmonsway, *The Anglo-Saxon Chronicle*, 2nd edn, London 1972, Introduction (pagination varies in different reprintings). The last annal written before there is a change in the shade of the ink used, and a change in the scribal hand, is against the row for the year 1073. But what seems to have escaped notice is that this annal records, in Old English, that 'In this year archbishop Lanfranc established [the primacy of] Christ Church [Canterbury] on 9 April [i.e. the day after Easter]', and that this event took place in 1072 (see below, p. 53), not 1073: the scribe has simply allowed his eye to drift as it traversed the double-page spread and consequently recorded this annal one line too low on the right-hand page.
[15]   Temple 1976 (as n. 1 above), pp. 115–7, no. 98.
[16]   T. A. Heslop, 'A Dated 'Late Anglo-Saxon' Illuminated Psalter', *Antiquaries Journal* 72, 1992, pp. 171–4. I am very grateful to Sandy Heslop for sending me a copy of his article prior to its publication while I was first working on a draft of this paper, and for stimulating discussion of a number of features of Arundel 60.

Though the manuscript was written about 1060, parts of it (folios 47–52 and 133–42v) are in an Anglo-Norman hand of the last quarter of the eleventh century. The script is contemporary with that of a charter of William the Conqueror in the British Museum (MS. Stowe 944, f. 41). Two of the illuminations of the second style immediately precede [*recte* follow] these folios, and another two (folios 13 and 53) are on pages where the interlinear Anglo-Saxon is in a different hand from that of the main part of the manuscript. It seems, therefore, that these illuminations were added – like the Anglo-Norman script – after the Conquest. They certainly show Norman influence.[17]

Taking in turn various points from Dodwell's analysis, it should first be noted that fols 47–52 (quire 6) and 133–142v (quires 17 & 18) are plainly not, as he implies by his use of the singular ('an Anglo-Norman hand'), all by the same scribe.[18] Folios 47–52 are a quire of six leaves which follow the end of Psalm 50 and contain an interpolated prayer based on each verse of that psalm whose inclusion seems to have always been intended, while fols 133–142 are two further quires which contain collects and prayers now interpolated between the end of the original litany and the collects.[19] Ker describes the work of these two scribes as of the second half of the eleventh century, and of the twelfth century, respectively;[20] and, although he does not mention this, a late eleventh- or early twelfth-century dating of the latter section is supported by the fact that the first of its two quires (quire 17, fols 133–136) is ruled in plummet rather than in blind, a practice found only rarely before the twelfth century.[21] Second, a minor point, the text of the charter copied into Stowe 944 at fol. 41r, datable to 1070, was probably copied into the volume at some time fairly soon thereafter, and does not necessarily support a date as late as *c*.1080.[22] Third, the 'interlinear Anglo-Saxon gloss ... in a different hand'[23]

---

[17]   See n. 9 above.

[18]   Wormald had already pointed this out, see F. Wormald, 'The English Saints in the Litany in Arundel MS. 60', *Analecta Bollandiana* 64, 1946, p. 72 and n. 4.

[19]   The first eight lines of the devotion are present, written by the original scribe, after the end of Psalm 50 on the last verso of the quire which precedes the interpolation of the whole devotion (fol. 46v).

[20]   Ker 1957 etc. (as n. 13 above), pp. 166–7, no. 134.

[21]   Ker describes the feature as being first introduced at Canterbury *c*.1100, see N. R. Ker, *English Manuscripts in the Century after the Norman Conquest*, Oxford 1960, p. 42. The second quire in this section is blind-ruled for more lines per page than were required in Arundel 60. This quire was presumably a pre-ruled 'left-over' from some other production.

[22]   The charter on fol. 41r is a grant by William I to Riwallon, abbot of the New Minster, see Keynes 1996 (as n. 3 above), pp. 101–2. Allowing for the difference in size (the script in the *Liber Vitae* being much smaller than in Arundel 60), the scribe of this charter is very probably the same as that of Arundel 60, fols 133–142, as claimed by Temple 1976 (as n. 1 above) p. 120, and Keynes 1996 (as n. 3 above), p. 102. Another addition to Stowe 944, on fol. 59, is a grant datable to

mentioned by Dodwell is another late eleventh- or early twelfth-century addition,[24] and thus does not relate to the date of the decoration of those pages. It is simply a result of the fact that the scribe of the main original Latin psalms text had left these pages blank so that the incipits could be executed in coloured display capitals, as indeed they later were, and the scribe of the rest of the Old English gloss (who was working before the decorator) had no way of knowing exactly where to place an interlinear gloss on pages where the main text itself had not yet been executed, therefore he left these pages blank, and the omission was not rectified until after the decoration had been supplied.[25]

I propose as an alternative that the two decorative 'campaigns' occurred not two decades apart but more or less contemporaneously, between five and ten years after the Conquest; the majority of the work being done in the 'Anglo-Saxon' style, with the project being brought to completion soon afterwards by others working in a more up-to-date 'Anglo-Norman' style. Such a hypothesis may be supported by the evidence of the red cross in the Easter table.

The problem of calculating the changing date of Easter and the movable feasts which depend upon it has always been crucial in the Church calendar. The calculation depends on both the lunar cycle of 19 days, and the solar cycle of 28 years, giving a sequence of 19 x 28 = 532 dates for Easter before

---

1082–87, also said by Temple and Keynes to be by the same scribe. This may well be true, in which case it is notable that his hand has become very markedly more angular in the intervening period, suggesting that the Arundel 60 additions are much closer in date to his c.1070 script than his 1082–87 script. It is significant for our purposes that Dodwell compares the script of the additions to Arundel 60 only with the c.1070 script in Stowe 944, and does not mention the 1082–87 script. Temple also states that the letter of Fulk added on fols 158r–160v of the Grimbald Gospels, London, British Lib. MS Add. 34890 (see Temple 1976 [as n. 1 above], pp. 86–8, no. 68), is also the work of the same scribe, but with this I cannot agree. There appear, in any case, to be misprints in Temple's text. At p. 87, describing the Grimbald Gosepls, she states that the letter from Fulk 'is a copy from the *second quarter of the 11th century* in the hand of the additions to ... Stowe 944 ... and Arundel 60' (my italics), but at p. 120, describing Arundel 60, she states that 'the additions of the *late 11th century* (ff. 133–42) ... are in the same hand as Fulk's letter ... and additions to ... Stowe 944' (my italics).

23   Curiously, Dodwell mentions this hand on fols 13 and 53, the beginnings of Psalms 1 and 51, but does not mention the same hand on fol. 85, the beginning of Psalm 101, suggesting further confusion in his text as printed.

24   Ker 1957 etc. (as n. 13 above), p. 167.

25   It is possible that the interlinear gloss was not originally intended, since the main text is not spaced out in anticipation of such a gloss; but this, as Richard Gameson kindly reminds me, is not uncommon among the several surviving Winchester Psalters with an interlinear gloss.

the cycle repeats itself.[26] In the Middle Ages various forms of Easter tables were therefore devised which allowed the user simply to look up the date from an existing list instead of having to go through complicated calculations each year. One of the most common forms of such lists is a table laid out in a grid of nineteen columns and twenty-eight rows, with a letter of the alphabet in each square of the grid, the squares of the grid representing the 532 years of the cycle, and the letters representing the date on which Easter falls in each year of the cycle.[27]

The potential use of marks in such tables for dating purposes has long been recognised. As E. W. B. Nicholson noted in 1905:

> It is common in these and similar tables to find dots and strokes: sometimes ... there are a number of them, and then they can merely show that the table was *used* about the dates indicated. But in others there is only a single mark at about the date when one would expect the MS. to have been written, and in such cases it is natural to suppose that the scribe deliberately marked the Easter next in front of him. [To this he added a footnote:] It may be suggested that the dot or stroke may mean a cancel, and that the Easter so marked is the last behind the scribe and not the next in front of him. I leave this an open question ...[28]

This sort of evidence must be used with care, of course, since there is always the danger of attempting to interpret what are, in reality, accidental or meaningless marks.[29] Thus, it will be necessary to ensure that any date derived from a mark in an Easter table does not conflict with other available indicators of date.

The first quire of the psalter is a gathering of twelve leaves, made up of six regular bifolia, in which the 'Anglo-Saxon' drawings are found. It contains calendrical and prognosticational material (fol. 1r–v), the calendar itself (fols 2r–7v),[30] and further calendrical material (fols 8r–12r). The full-page

[26] An explanation of the details may be found in Günzel 1993 (as n. 12 above), pp. 16ff.

[27] For perhaps the clearest explanation of the layout of such Easter tables, see L. Delisle, *Notice de douze livres royaux de XIIe et du XIVe siècle*, Paris 1902, pp. 102–4; reprinted in H. Martin, *Psautier de Saint Louis et de Blanche de Castille* (Les Joyaux de l'Arsenal, 1), Paris n.d., pp. 14–7, referring to pl. XIV.

[28] Nicholson's remarks are in F. Madan, *A Summary Catalogue of Western Manuscripts in the Bodleian Library at Oxford, V: (Collections Received During the Second Half of the 19th Century and Miscellaneous MSS. Acquired Between 1695 and 1890) Nos. 24331–31000*, Oxford 1905, pp. xii–xiii.

[29] H. M. Bannister, 'Signs in Kalendarial Tables', in *Mélanges offerts à M. Emile Chatelain par ses élèves et ses amis*, Paris 1910, pp. 141–9, presents the most extensive list of manuscripts which have been dated in this way but he suggests caution in treating 'signs' in calendrical tables, since they are sometimes no more than smudges, pinpricks, or other accidental marks, rather than deliberate scribal notations.

Crucifixion in 'Anglo-Saxon' style is on the final verso (fol. 12v) of this gathering, whose writing is contemporary with the rest of the original psalter.[31]

The penultimate page of the calendrical material, fol. 11v, is occupied by an Easter table (Fig. 3). Here the grid consists of 28 rows, as usual, but only 11 columns of letters;[32] it thus does not represent the full cycle of 532 years. The letters in the grid each represent one of the possible dates on which Easter may fall, using the Roman alphabet (omitting J, V and W) plus ω (omega) in black ink, and further letters in red to make up the 35 different symbols necessary to indicate the 35 possible dates for Easter which may fall on any day from March 22 to April 25.[33] These 35 letters are also set out alongside the dates which they represent in the calendar itself, next to the last ten days of March and the first 25 days of April (fol. 3r–v), to the left of the usual columns of Golden Numbers, Dominical Letters, etc.[34]

With the aid of a list of the dates on which Easter fell during the Middle Ages,[35] one can quickly find out that the letters in the table are those necessary for finding the date of Easter for the years 1060 to 1367.[36] We can safely assume, therefore, that such a table would have been of no practical use before the ecclesiastical year immediately prior to Easter 1060, and this therefore provides a firm *terminus post quem* of Easter (April 4) 1059 for the writing of the table. Generally, as has been mentioned, full Easter tables of this type are composed of 28 rows, as here (for the 28-year solar cycle), in 19 columns (for the 19-day lunar cycle), but the fact that the scribe of Arundel 60 gives only 11 columns of Easter dates suggests that he was copying from an exemplar of which the first eight columns were, by the date he was writing, redundant. Naturally enough, he spared himself the tedium of copying out unnecessary columns of letters, and started his copy with the column containing the date of Easter for the year in which he was writing.[37] Thus, even if there was no other evidence on which to base a date, we could be

30 The text is printed in F. Wormald, *English Kalendars Before A.D. 1100* (Henry Bradshaw Society, 72), London 1934, pp. 142–53, no. 11.

31 Ker 1957 etc. (as n. 13 above), p. 167.

32 The two leftmost columns contain the letter 'B', in every fourth row, to indicate leap years (B is short for 'bissextus', because in a leap year the sixth day before the kalends of March, i.e. 24 February, was counted twice); and the numbers 'i'–'vii', for the concurrents.

33 See Table 1 for the letters and the dates to which they refer.

34 See Martin n.d. (as n. 27 above), pls. IV–V.

35 See, for example, C. R. Cheney, *Handbook of Dates for Students of English History* (Royal Historical Society Guides and Handbooks, 4), London 1945, repr. 1991, pp. 156–9.

36 See Table 1.

37 For possible evidence that he was copying from an exemplar whose script gave him some trouble, see the note appended to Table 1.

confident that the writing of the psalter took place within the first 19-year cycle provided by the table, i.e. 1059/60–1078/9. This is perfectly in accord with the traditional date of c.1060 for the writing of the main psalter texts. But is it possible to be more specific about which year within this period the scribe worked?

Half way down the first column, in the row for the year 1073, is the letter 'h', in black ink, which represents the date March 31.[38] Next to this letter 'h' is inscribed a cross in red ink, in exactly the same deep red colour as is used for various letters in the table (being less orange in tone than the red ink used for ruling the grid of the table itself). It is the only such cross in the entire table, and it seems reasonable to suggest that when the table was written out, this mark served to indicate the starting point for the use of the table, flagging either the preceding or the following Easter, which would mean that the table was written between Easter (April 8) 1072 and Easter (April 20) 1074.

Attractive as this suggestion may seem, neatly supplying a date roughly half-way between c.1160 and c.1180, one has to admit that, despite the apparently identical red ink used, it is impossible to state with absolute certainty that the red cross was made at the same time as the writing of the rest of the manuscript. But if not at that date, when might it have been made? If we pursue, for a moment, the accepted hypothesis that the psalter was written and decorated in two separate stages, a possible alternative is the date when the psalter was finally completed and made fit for use by the provision of its 'Anglo-Norman' decoration. But in that case the 'c.1080' decoration is in fact perhaps as early as 1072. And if this is indeed the true date of the 'c.1080' campaign, which has thus hitherto been dated about a decade too late, could it not also be that the 'c.1060' work has hitherto been dated too early by about the same amount? A date of 1072–4 for both the 'c.1060' and the 'c.1080' work should be perfectly acceptable in light of the post-Conquest dating of the Caligula and Tiberius manuscripts mentioned above, and it eliminates the need for supposing that the Arundel Psalter remained 'unfinished' for two decades.

As mentioned earlier, one must be very careful to ensure that a date derived from a mark in an Easter table is in accord with other dating evidence. We may briefly therefore introduce into the discussion questions of iconography and technique, because together they offer supportive evidence for a post-Conquest date for the whole book. In 1954, the same year that Dodwell's influential argument for two separate campaigns appeared, Rickert's seminal study of medieval British painting was published.[39] She too describes Arundel 60 as 'made for the New Minster [Winchester] c.1060', but

---

[38]   See the note following Table 1.

[39]   M. Rickert, *Painting in Britain: The Middle Ages* (The Pelican History of Art), London 1954, 2nd ed., 1965.

because, like Wormald,[40] she envisaged Continental influence present in England before the Conquest, she does not insist that the fully-painted 'Anglo-Norman' work is necessarily significantly later than the drawings, merely suggesting 'two different hands, one perhaps later than the other'.[41] Describing the line-drawn *Crucifixion*, she ingeniously proposes that:

> The Christ in this miniature seems to have been taken, with some adaptation, from the Christ of the Crucifixion in Tib.C.vi (fol. 12 verso [*recte* fol. 13 recto]); the Virgin from Mary Magdalene of the Three Marys at the Tomb (fol. 13 verso);[42] and John from an angel above the arches of the Easter Table on fol. 3.[43]

If this idea has any merit, it is significant that the source for these figures, Cotton Tiberius C. vi, thought by her to be 'of about the middle of the eleventh century'[44] has now been shown to have a firm *terminus post quem* of 1064, and is in all probability post-Conquest.[45] Thus if the so-called '*c*.1060' decoration of Arundel 60 derives in some way from Tiberius C. vi, the former must also be after 1064 and, in all likelihood, post-Conquest.

Turning to technique, Dormer has recently proposed, in the only in-depth study of drawing techniques in English medieval manuscripts, that the drawings of Arundel 60 show a later development of a 'general hardening of style' of which an earlier stage can be seen in Tiberius C. vi.[46] This further suggests that Arundel 60 may be later than the Tiberius Psalter. Thus, there are several forms of evidence in support of the hypothesis that the 'Anglo-Saxon' decoration was executed after the Conquest, and it seems that it may indeed be valid to interpret the cross in the Easter table of Arundel 60 as reliable dating evidence. And if 1073 plus-or-minus one year is an acceptable answer to the question of *when* the psalter was made, then it is worth re-examining the questions of *where* and *for whom* it was written in the light of this newly-proposed date.

There were three Benedictine houses in Winchester: the monastic cathedral, or Old Minster; the abbey, or New Minster; and the house of nuns, or Nunnaminster. Although most scholars state that the book was probably

---

40 See n. 8 above.
41 Rickert 1954 (as n. 39 above), p. 63.
42 It may also be noted that the figure of Virgo in the calendar of Arundel 60 is a mirror-image of Mary of the Crucifixion; the similarities extend to most of the individual drapery-folds, except at the bottom hem, and the only significant differences are that Virgo does not have Mary's halo, and the book in her hand has been swapped for a sort of flaming horn.
43 Rickert 1965 (as n. 39 above), p. 63.
44 Ibid., p. 62.
45 See n. 16 above.
46 S. E. Dormer, 'Drawings in English Manuscripts c.950–c.1385: Technique and Purpose', Ph.D. diss., University of London, Courtauld Institute of Art 1991, p. 80.

made for the New Minster, on the evidence that several New Minster saints are emphasised in the calendar,[47] it should be remembered that the litany places Old Minster saints far higher up the ranking than New Minster ones.[48] The Nunnaminster can probably be ruled out because its saints are not sufficiently highly ranked in either calendar or litany and there is no other explicit evidence that the book was intended for female use. But perhaps any attempt to decide between the two other foundations is an artificial one. Until the New Minster was moved outside the city walls and renamed Hyde Abbey in the early twelfth century it stood within the precincts of the cemetery of the Old Minster – they were just yards apart – and it would therefore not be surprising to find that saints whose relics belonged to one house were venerated in a devotional book owned by someone from the neighbouring house.[49] Discussing the origin of the psalter Turner judiciously suggests that 'It should most probably be associated not with a place but with a person, and personal piety is reflected in the eclecticism of the calendar and litany.'[50] So who might this person have been?

Just as one must be careful not to over-interpret a mark in an Easter table, one must be careful about making links between observed phenomena in a manuscript and historical facts which might, in truth, be unrelated. But if we *were* to indulge in speculation, it would be very tempting to see links between the revised dating, further features of the psalter, and contemporary historical events. In 1070 Stigand had been deprived both of the archbishopric of Canterbury and of the bishopric of Winchester; at Canterbury he was replaced by Lanfranc and at Winchester by Walkelin. Walkelin is thus one possible candidate for the role of first owner of the psalter, since it was started within a few years of his coming to the see. An Old Minster-Walkelin link with the psalter is further suggested by the presence of a leaf bound in at the back of the volume, whose writing can be dated securely to the year 1099.[51]

[47]　See Wormald 1934 (as n. 30 above).

[48]　Wormald 1946 (as n. 18 above); M. Lapidge, *Anglo-Saxon Litanies of the Saints* (Henry Bradshaw Society, 106), London 1991, pp. 68, 142–7; Sisam and Sisam 1959 (as n. 11 above), p. 58 n. 3, observe that one of the petitions after the litany of saints in Arundel 60 starts 'Ut episcopum nostrum ...', while the same petition in the earlier New Minster book, British Library, Cotton MS. Titus D. xxvi, starts 'Ut episcopum et abbatem nostrum ...'; but as with the litany and calendar, such details probably tell us more about the source of the text in front of the scribe, rather than the house for which he was making a copy.

[49]　For the locations of the two houses see the maps in *Winchester in the Early Middle Ages: an Edition of the Winton Domesday* (Winchester Studies, 1), M. Biddle (ed.), Oxford 1976, fig. 9 (fold-out maps facing p. 328).

[50]　*The Golden Age of Anglo-Saxon Art 966–1066*, J. Backhouse, D. H. Turner and L. Webster (eds), London 1984, p. 83.

[51]　The volume was in an eighteenth-century binding when Ker described it in 1957 (as n. 13 above), but was re-bound by the British Museum in 1966, and since the

On the verso of this leaf is a list of the bishops (not abbots) of Winchester, in which the last name is Walkelin's.[52] It is highly suggestive that Walkelin died in 1098, and that this leaf was written perhaps just a few months later. The leaf, which marks a specific moment in time, could therefore be interpreted as a sort of memorial to Walkelin, an appropriate addition to a book which he had owned for almost the entire duration of his long Winchester episcopacy. There is, however, an equally likely alternative.

At Easter 1072, Lanfranc held a synod at Winchester, which deposed Wulfric, abbot of the New Minster, and he was succeeded later the same year by Riwallon.[53] If the psalter was indeed made for use at the New Minster, as so many scholars have stated, then here is another possible candidate for its first owner, for again we find a remarkable coincidence of dates: the earliest possible date for the Easter table in Arundel 60 is Easter 1072, and within months of this date Riwallon became abbot of the New Minster.

---

older binding was not preserved, it is perhaps now impossible to ascertain the precise original physical relationship between this single leaf and the rest of the volume. It is possible that the leaf was inserted at the same time as the insertion of fols 133–142 (dated by Ker to the twelfth century, and by Wormald to the late eleventh century). There is no reason to doubt that it was always bound into the present volume, and that it was always the final leaf: in the thirteenth century someone wrote an ownership inscription on the verso: 'Istud salterium est domini Iohannes [remainder illegible]'.

[52] The recto contains Latin and Old English versions of the Six Ages of the World, in which the period since the Nativity of Christ is stated to be 1099 years. In addition, the list of bishops on the verso includes Walkelin (d. 1098), but does not include William Giffard, who became bishop in 1100.

[53] For a list of abbots and their dates, see W. Dugdale, *Monasticon Anglicanum: a History of the Abbies and other Monasteries, Hospitals, Frieries and Cathedral and Collegiate Churches, with their Dependencies, in England and Wales ... a New Edition...*, London 1819, reprinted Westmead, Hants 1970, vol. II, p. 431; and Keynes 1996 (as n. 3 above), p. 91.

Table 1: Possible dates of Easter, and their corresponding letter
in the calendar of Arundel 60, fol. 3r–v.

Mar 22 A	Apr 1 *N*	Apr 11 Q	
Mar 23 B	Apr 2 I	Apr 12 R	Apr 21 *B*
Mar 24 C	Apr 3 k	Apr 13 S	Apr 22 *C*
Mar 25 D	Apr 4 L	Apr 14 T	Apr 23 *k*
Mar 26 *D*	Apr 5 M	Apr 15 V	Apr 24 *L*
Mar 27 E	Apr 6 *M*	Apr 16 *V*	Apr 25 ω
Mar 28 *E*	Apr 7 N	Apr 17 x	
Mar 29 F	Apr 8 O	Apr 18 y	
Mar 30 G	Apr 9 P	Apr 19 Z	
Mar 31 h	Apr 10 Q	Apr 20 *A*	
(see note below)			

Italic letters indicate those in red ink in the manuscript; the remainder appear in black ink.

Note:

I have attempted to emulate the appearance of the original letter-forms of the scribe, which is why a few letters (h, k, x, and y) appear as lower-case letters, and the rest as upper case (compare, for example, the letter 'h' in the inscription 'IOhANNES' in Fig. 1).

In the calendar (fol. 3r–v) the letter 'h' is written next to March 31, and '*N*' next to April 1; but in the table, while '*N*' does indeed represent April 1, 'N' represents March 31 several times. The sequence of the letters, as laid out above, which essentially follows the alphabet through from A to Z in sequence, with various letters repeated in red, would lead us to expect not 'N' and '*N*' but 'h' and '*h*' for March 31 and April 1 (occurring as they do between E, F, G, and I, K, L). It thus seems likely that the exemplar was written in a minuscule script, quite possibly with short ascenders, which caused the scribe to mistake 'h' for 'n' in the majority of cases. However, the fact that the year 1073 is the only instance in the table in which the scribe uses the letter 'h' correctly for March 31 – indeed, it looks as if it has been corrected over an erasure – adds substance to my supposition that this was an important year which the scribe took special care to get right.

'A Very Old Book': The Burdett Psalter-Hours, Made for a Thirteenth-Century Hospitaller

JANET BACKHOUSE

The pessimists who tell us that no significant illuminated manuscripts remain to be discovered are proved wrong with encouraging frequency. The book which I am about to describe emerged from a battered cardboard box one September afternoon in 1978. It had been brought in to the British Library's Department of Manuscripts by a rather elegant retired senior officer of the RAF, who explained that it had been an heirloom in an English landed family for some three centuries and was currently being looked after by his wife. An old label attached to the box read: 'Very Old Book bequeathed by Jane Burdett 1694', which was apparently the sum of their factual knowledge about it. The quality of the manuscript was clear from the first glimpse of one of its five full-page miniatures, as was the fact that it was made a good four hundred years earlier than the date on the label. The visitor was happy to deposit it in the Library for further investigation and there it was to remain in almost complete confidentiality for nearly twenty years while successive owners, now fully aware of its value and interest, tried to make up their minds about its future. The short paper which I gave at St Andrews was the first public acknowledgement of its existence. A few months later its guardians decided to put it on the open market and it was scheduled for sale at Sotheby's on 23 June 1998.[1]

The manuscript itself is a very handsome psalter-hours, illuminated in a leading Parisian workshop probably during the 1280s.[2] This type of book,

---

[1]   I am grateful to my original visitor and his wife for entrusting the manuscript to me for examination and for allowing me to have record photographs made. These are used in the present paper. I am also grateful to the subsequent owners for permission to make the book public. Both sets of owners have preferred to remain anonymous. The manuscript is detailed as lot 50 in Sotheby's sale of *Western Manuscripts and Miniatures*, London, 23 June 1998, with a separate catalogue copiously illustrated in colour. It was bought anonymously with a hammer price of £2.75 million.

[2]   See the exhibition catalogue *L'art au temps des rois maudits, Philippe le Bel et ses fils, 1285–1328*, Paris 1998, pp. 267–8. I am extremely grateful to François Avril for

combining the two standard texts of personal devotion, enjoyed considerable popularity during the late thirteenth and the fourteenth centuries, at the time when the book of hours was achieving a general ascendancy over the psalter as a focus of private daily prayer. Examples are to be found on both sides of the Channel and in England at least continued to attract patronage over a very long period. A number of the manuscripts commissioned for members of the Bohun family combine psalter and hours, as does the magnificent English prayerbook made during the second decade of the fifteenth century for John, Duke of Bedford.[3] The original owner of the 'Very Old Book' is portrayed several times within its pages, once as a suppliant at the feet of the saint in a full-page miniature of the Baptist and four times as a marginal figure alongside historiated initials at major divisions of the text. He wears the black robes of a Hospitaller, with their eight-pointed white cross on his shoulder, but there is unfortunately no further clue, either written or symbolic, to his identity. If the illuminator is to be believed, he was no longer young. He must certainly have been a person of substance to command a book of this calibre. It is possible that St John the Baptist was a personal patron, indicating that he was probably called Jean or John, but the saint was also the general patron of the Hospitaller Order, so the devotion may merely be a corporate one. Furthermore it must be said that his nationality is also ambiguous. Though the illumination of the manuscript is undoubtedly French, its patron could theoretically have come from any European nation, as the Hospitallers were an international order and its members, especially those in its higher ranks, travelled extensively between Europe and the Holy Land.

The manuscript, which measures approximately 235mm by 155mm, contains 106 leaves of vellum, substantially arranged in gatherings of 12 (with catchwords) except at the beginning and the end, where gatherings of unequal length are provided to carry such special elements as the calendar and the full-page miniatures and to accommodate the final passages of text.[4] The text comprises a calendar (fols 1–6v), prayers for use before the psalter (fols 12v–13v), the psalms (fols 14–70v) and canticles (fols 71–76), the hours of the Virgin (fols 77–89v), the penitential psalms and litany (fols 90–95v), the office of the dead (fols 96–106) and an added office of the Passion on fol.106r and 106v.

---

sharing with me his knowledge of the illuminator responsible for the miniatures in the manuscript.

[3] See L. F. Sandler, *Gothic Manuscripts, 1285–1385* (A Survey of Manuscripts Illuminated in the British Isles, J. J. G. Alexander [ed.], vol. 5), London 1986, nos. 135, 138, 142 and (related) 145; K. L. Scott, *Later Gothic Manuscripts, 1390–1490* (A Survey of Manuscripts Illuminated in the British Isles, J. J. G. Alexander [ed.], vol. 6), London 1996, no. 54.

[4] The manuscript has never been foliated. Details of its structure are offered in Sotheby's catalogue description (as n. 1 above).

The calendar, written in red and black and apparently very selective, is surprisingly uninformative. The majority of the red entries record the feastdays of apostles or of saints universally commemorated. The same is true of the handful of vigils and octaves entered, other than those for such obvious celebrations as Christmas or the Assumption. A number of comparatively recent feasts appear, namely St Dominic (d. 1221) on 5 August, with the translation of his relics in 1233 in red on 24 May;[5] St Francis (d. 1226) on 4 October; St Elizabeth of Thuringia on 19 November, as established in 1235; and St Peter Martyr, canonised in 1253, on 29 April. Two feasts can be regarded as possibly linking the book with Parisian practice. The Crown of Our Lord (the Crown of Thorns) is commemorated on 4 May and the Exaltation of the Holy Cross on 14 September, a feast of great antiquity, is picked out by the insertion of a little cross with red dots in its angles. Both are specifically associated with St Louis's acquisition of the relics of the Passion in or around 1241. Indeed, he personally carried the relic of the True Cross in procession on the appropriate day in that year. The manuscript is of course too early to allow for the inclusion of St Louis himself, canonised only in 1297. Among early additions to the calendar it is surprising to see the ancient feast of the Invention of the Cross supplied at 3 May, given the ownership of the manuscript. There are no especially notable French names among the saints. However, in addition to the predictable Thomas Becket, Bishop (sic) of Canterbury, in red on 29 December, England contributes 'Odouardi confessor' on 13 October, Edmund King and Martyr in red on 20 November, and Edmund Archbishop (that is, St Edmund Rich, canonised in 1246 and with strong French links) as an early addition on 16 November. The litany, which was heavily revised and greatly expanded during the fifteenth century, includes Edmund and Thomas at the end of the martyrs and the second Edmund in third place among the confessors, all in the original hand.

Like the litany, the texts of the hours and of the office of the dead were revised during the fifteenth century, in order to bring them into line with current Sarum use. These revisions are heavier in the latter than in the former. In the hours, although two leaves were added to the structure of the book in order to allow for the addition of a series of memorials of saints after lauds as favoured in English practice,[6] with contingent erasure and re-insertion of about a page of the original text, only one substantial alteration is to be noted. The capitulum at lauds has been removed and replaced with the Sarum choice

[5]   In the entry on 24 May he is designated 'Beatus', the translation having taken place in 1233, a year before his formal canonisation.
[6]   The saints for whom memorials were provided are Michael, John the Baptist, Peter and Paul, Stephen, John the Evangelist, Lawrence, and Thomas Becket (cancelled in the sixteenth century); with George, Christopher, Denis, Blaise, Eustace, Katherine, Margaret, Barbara, Martha and Ursula listed in a single petition; then Nicolas, Katherine and Margaret, Anne, Relics and Peace.

57

of 'Maria virgo semper letare'. It should be borne in mind that the text of the various uses familiar from later books was by no means completely determined at this early date in its development.[7] However, the hours here do apparently follow the Sarum pattern from the outset and certainly differ substantially from the text found in British Lib. MS Add. 41061, which was identified by Leroquais as being of Hospitaller use, using for comparison MS lat. 1400 in the Bibliothèque nationale in Paris.[8]

Several scribes contributed to the completed manuscript. The main original hand, which may be seen in Figs 7–13, produced a clear and competent but not particularly distinguished liturgical script, with rubrics in red and alternating text initials in red and blue with contrasting penwork. A slightly less polished contemporary wrote out the second portion of the office of the dead (fols 103–6). The prayers for use before the psalter, which fill the second, third and fourth pages of a bifolio added to the original structure immediately in front of the 'Beatus' page (fols 12–13), are an early, apparently more or less contemporary addition by two distinct scribes, the second of whom uses a very handsome italianate hand.[9] The fifteenth-century additions and corrections are readily distinguishable from all these early contributions, though their scribe seems to have taken some pains to avoid appearing too incompatible with them.

The illumination of the manuscript, comprising five full-page miniatures and a series of historiated and decorated initials, is in a class superior to that of its scripts. Each of the eight liturgical divisions of the psalter is marked by a large historiated initial of an appropriate, and indeed by this date traditional, subject, as follows:

[7]   Comparison of the texts in the two dozen English books of hours listed in J. Backhouse, *The Madresfield Hours* (Roxburghe Club), Oxford 1975, pp. 30–3, revealed some degree of variation in virtually every case.

[8]   See Leroquais's letter in London, British Lib. MS Add. 43688 Y. For the Paris manuscript see V. Leroquais, *Les Livres d'heures manuscrits de la Bibliothèque nationale*, 3 vols, Paris 1927, vol. 1, p. 232.

[9]   The first of the prayers: 'Deus ineffabilis misericordie, deus immense pietatis, deus conditor...', is a variant on the prayer beginning: 'Deus inaesteimabilis...', composed by Alcuin for Charlemagne, see V. Leroquais, *Les Psautiers manuscrits latins des bibliothèques publiques de France*, 3 vols, Paris 1940–41, vol. 1, pp. 23, 25. It was adopted by Anselm and appears in British Lib. MS Royal 8 B. i, fol. 50v, see G. F. Warner and J. P. Gilson, *A Catalogue of Western Manuscripts in the Old Royal and Kings Collections*, London 1921, vol. 1, p. 218. The two shorter prayers: 'Suscipere dignare domine omnipotens hos psalmos consecratos...' and 'Aufer a me domine illusiones spirituum...' occur in the early thirteenth-century Westminster Psalter (British Lib. MS Royal 2 A. xxii, fol. 11r, see Warner and Gilson, vol. 1, p. 36, and in the Canterbury Psalter of similar date in Paris (Bibl. nationale MS lat. 8846), see Leroquais 1940–41, p. 78.

fol.14r: David playing the harp (Psalm 1, 'Beatus vir'; Fig. 7)
fol. 22v: David pointing to his eyes (Psalm 26, 'Dominus illuminatio')
fol. 28v: David pointing to his mouth (Psalm 38, 'Dixi custodiam')
fol. 34r: the fool (Psalm 52, 'Dixit insipiens'; Fig. 8)
fol. 39v: David calling upon God (Psalm 68, 'Salvum me fac')
fol. 46r: David playing the bells (Psalm 80, 'Exultate deo')
fol. 52r: three priests at a lectern, singing from what appears to be a
           text provided with neums[10] (Psalm 97, 'Cantate domino'; Fig. 9)
fol. 58r: the Holy Trinity (Psalm 109, 'Dixit dominum'; Fig. 10)

The hours of the Virgin are introduced by an initial containing the figures of the Virgin and Child enthroned (fol. 77r: 'Domine labia mea'; Fig. 11). The seven divisions of the hours (lauds, prime, terce, sext, none, vespers and compline) are distinguished by decorative initials, with gothic interlace and ivy leaf designs, occasionally extended into the margins. The pentitential psalms open with an initial enclosing God the Father enthroned, carrying an orb representing the world (fol. 90r: 'Domine ne in furore'; Fig. 12) and the office of the dead begins with an initial showing two priests officiating beside a draped coffin flanked by candles (fol. 96r: 'Dilexi quoniam'; Fig. 13). On fols 14, 77, 90 and 96 (i.e. at the beginning of each of the main portions of the text) the kneeling figure of the original Hospitaller patron is placed in the margin, alongside the left hand edge of the historiated initial.

The artistic glory of the manuscript lies in its full-page miniatures, which are placed between the end of the calendar and the opening of the psalter. They occupy what was originally a discrete gathering of six leaves, now lacking the fifth leaf. The verso of the first of these leaves (fol. 76r) carries the miniature of the patron kneeling at the feet of John the Baptist (Fig. 1). The saint is dressed in a surcoat of skins over a brown robe and carries an orb charged with an image of the Lamb of God. On the diapered background, white fleurs de lys on blue alternate with panels of burnished gold. A blank recto is followed by a fully illustrated double opening of infancy episodes, arranged in eight compartments. On fol. 8v (Fig. 2) the subjects are the Annunciation, the Visitation, the Annunciation to the Shepherds, and the Nativity. On fol. 9r (Fig. 3) we see the Adoration of the Magi, the Presentation, the Flight into Egypt, and the Massacre of the Innocents. The next two pages (fols 9v and 10r) are again blank, followed by a series of Passion scenes. On fol. 10v (Fig. 4) four compartments house the Betrayal, Christ before Pilate, the Flagellation and the Carrying of the Cross. On fol. 11r (Fig. 5) the page is divided horizontally into two to show very similar compositions representing the Ascension and Pentecost. Between fols 10 and 11 a visible stub indicates the missing fifth leaf of the gathering. This must

---

[10]   The inclusion of real music in miniatures of this type is discussed by C. Page, 'An English Motet of the 14th Century in Performance: Two Contemporary Images', *Early Music* 25, 1997, pp. 7–32.

have carried miniatures of the Crucifixion and the Resurrection, which are noticeably absent from the existing cycle, though there is nothing to indicate whether they were treated as whole page subjects or whether additional episodes such as the Harrowing of Hell were included.

The gathering dedicated to these New Testament subjects is succeeded, as noted above, by a single bifolio carrying on its latter pages the added prayers for use before the psalms. Its first page (fol. 12r; Fig. 6) is however devoted to an unpainted drawing in ink of the figures of four well-known saints, Lawrence with his gridiron, Stephen with his stones, Margaret with her dragon and Catherine with her wheel. These are arranged in four compartments, with quatrefoils at the corners of the frame, just as in the other miniatures. Given the difference in medium, it is hard to assess whether these are coeval with the rest of the decoration of the manuscript. However, if there is a difference in date, it must be a very minor one.

On stylistic grounds, the miniatures in this exceptionally beautiful manuscript can be attributed to one of the leading Parisian book painters of the last quarter of the thirteenth century. His identity has yet to be established and he is known for convenience as the Méliacin Master, in tribute to the finest work previously attributed to him, in a handsome copy of Girart d'Amiens's romance of Méliacin now in the Bibliothèque nationale in Paris.[11] A very substantial list of manuscripts attributable to him has been compiled, including a number of notable secular works as well as liturgical ones, and his identifiable clientele embraces numerous members of the French royal family as well as figures from their court.[12] He was clearly the principal court illuminator in the period immediately preceding the emergence of Honoré. The present manuscript ranks among his most ambitious and successful works and its original patron must indeed have been a person of high standing.

Commemorative entries added to the calendar of the manuscript show that it had passed into ownership in England within the first couple of decades of its history. There it has remained until the present day. There are seven of these entries, written in several different hands but all relating to persons connected with eastern England in the years immediately before 1300, as follows:

22 May:	'Obitus domine dyonisie de monte caniso'
25 August:	'Obitus R. Comitis Oxon.'
25 September:	'Obitus domini Walteri de Redesham'
3 October:	'Obitus domine matilde de crek'
16 November:	'Obitus magistri Willelmi Coci. p.'
23 November:	'Obitus domini Johannes de Redeswelle'

[11] Paris, Bibl. nationale MS fr. 1633, in *L'art au temps des rois maudits* (as n. 2 above), no. 174.

[12] For manuscripts ascribed to him see, P. Stirnemann, 'Fils de la Vierge 1140–1314', *Revue de l'Art* 90, 1990, p. 73 no. 44.

15 December: 'Obitus Domini Willelmi de Garenne.'

The first of these entries refers to Denise de Munchensy, who died in 1304. Hers is in fact the latest of the deaths recorded. She was the widow of Warin de Munchensy (d. 1255), whom she had married as her second husband in 1234-5. Warin had also been twice married. His first wife was one of the five daughters of William Marshal, Earl of Pembroke (d. 1219), and she subsequently became co-heir of her brother Anselm. The daughter of this marriage, Joan de Munchensy, married William de Valence, uterine half-brother of Henry III, who acquired the Pembroke title in right of his wife. Denise's own son, William de Munchensy, was killed at the siege of Dryslwyn Castle in 1287, leaving an infant daughter also named Denise as his heir. Her marriage was granted in 1290 to Hugh de Vere, second son of Robert de Vere, Earl of Oxford. The marriage took place in 1294, presumably as soon as the bride reached canonical age, she having been until then under the guardianship of her grandmother.[13]

Denise the elder was almost certainly the 'ma dame Dyonise de Mountechensi' to whom Walter de Bibbesworth addressed his treatise on the French language (a rhyming French vocabulary designed to teach children appropriate terms of husbandry and management for use in later life) about the middle of the thirteenth century.[14] She was also the foundress of the Franciscan nunnery at Waterbeach, near Cambridge, to which she brought Minoresses from the continent in 1294.[15] The community was refounded in the following century at Denny by Marie de St Pol, widow of Aymer de Valence, Earl of Pembroke, who had succeeded to the Munchensy properties through his mother Joan, when the younger Denise died childless in 1313.[16]

Robert de Vere, Earl of Oxford, father of Denise's husband Hugh and commemorated on 25 August, died in 1296. William de Warenne, recorded on 15 December, was his son-in-law, husband of his daughter Joan (d. 1293) and therefore potentially brother-in-law of Hugh and Denise. William was the son of John de Warenne, Earl of Surrey, and his wife, Alice de Valence, sister of William, Earl of Pembroke and thus sister-in-law of Joan de Munchensy. He died in 1286, apparently the victim of an ambush on the occasion of a tournament at Croydon, predeceasing his father by almost twenty years.

Matilda de Crek, entered on 3 October, is probably an error for Margery de Crek, who died in or about 1283.[17] Like the elder Denise de Munchensy,

---

13   Most of the family details which follow are drawn from G. E. Cockayne, *The Complete Peerage*, 12 vols, London 1910-59, which includes entries for the Munchensy family, Hugh de Vere, and the Earls of Oxford and Pembroke.

14   M. T. Clanchy, *From Memory to Written Record*, London 1979, pp. 151-4.

15   Victoria County History, *Cambridgeshire*, vol. 2, London 1967, pp. 292-5.

16   Ibid., pp. 295-7.

17   M. W. Labarge, *A Baronial Household of the Thirteenth Century*, London 1965, pp. 49-50. The connection of Margery's husband with William Marshal is noted.

she was a widow for a long period during the later years of her life. Her husband, Bartholomew de Crek (of North Creake in Norfolk), died during the 1250s and soon afterwards Margery founded the Augustinian nunnery at Flixton in Suffolk. There is some evidence of intermarriage between the de Crek, the de Vere and the de Munchensy families and all certainly came from the same social circles and had links in the same parts of the country.[18]

Of the remaining three commemorations one, that of Walter de Redesham (25 September), can be linked with Margery de Crek. He was one of the witnesses to the foundation charter of Flixton and later makes similar appearances in other documents relating to the house.[19] He took his name from Redisham in Suffolk and he died in 1291.[20] John de Redeswelle (23 November) was apparently an associate of Denise de Munchensy senior, taking his name from the manor of Ridgwell in Essex which was one of the properties that came to her from her first husband, Walter Langton (d. 1234).[21] John, son of Eudo of Redeswell, is named as one of her attorneys when she travelled overseas in 1271.[22] A man of the same name, doubtless a representative of the next generation, appears in the service of Marie de St Pol in 1325-6.[23] Only Master William Coc p[resbiter] on 15 December remains unaccounted for. He could have been a personal priest or confessor.

Who was responsible for having these names entered into the calendar of this manuscript is not indicated. The timespan which they cover and the fairly close-knit nature of the group certainly suggest that the manuscript was in use in England by the end of the 13th century, only a very short time after its production. It is interesting to note that one of the prayers for use before the psalter (fol. 13v) has been provided between the lines with alternative endings for female use. Candidates for ownership at this time must certainly be the

---

[18] Margery's grandmother may have been a de Vere. William de Munchensy I of the elder branch of the family (d. circa 1263) was married to Margery's granddaughter Joan, daughter and heir of her son Geoffrey, Cockayne 1910–59 (as n. 13 above), IX, p. 415; C. Moor, *The Knights of Edward I*, London 1929–32, vol. 1, p. 246.

[19] For Flixton see Victoria County History, *Suffolk*, vol. 2, London 1907, p. 115. Stowe Charters 291–381 in the British Library relate to Flixton; Walter de Redesham appears as a witness in nos. 291, 304, 361, 365 and 376.

[20] For an outline of his career see Moor 1929–32 (as n. 18 above), vol. 4, p. 115. See also *Calendar of Inquisitions Post Mortem*, vol. 3, London 1912, p. 34.

[21] Walter was apparently a brother of Archbishop Stephen Langton, see Victoria County History, *Cambridgeshire*, vol. 2, London 1967, p. 292. Denise gave the advowson of the church to her foundation at Waterbeach in 1296 (ibid. p. 293).

[22] *Calendar of Patent Rolls: Henry III, 1266–1272*, London 1913, p. 599.

[23] *Calendar of Patent Rolls: Edward II, vol. 5: 1324–1327*, London 1904, pp. 200, 313. A Thomas de Redeswell also appears as attorney for Denise de Munchensy in 1294 and 1299 and as attorney for the Abbess of Waterbeach in 1298, at the instance of Hugh de Vere (*Calendar of Patent Rolls: Edward I, 1292–1301*, London 1895, pp. 99, 54 and 345 respectively).

younger Denise and her husband Hugh de Vere, who was apparently some twenty years her senior and thus more likely than she to remember some of the older people commemorated. This is, however, only conjecture.

It is clear from the amendments and additions to the text that the manuscript remained in England throughout the Middle Ages. The removal of the devotion to Becket in the memorials of the saints is witness to its continued presence during the Reformation. By the beginning of the seventeenth century it had passed into the hands of Anthony Hutton, counsellor at law and a master of the High Court of Chancery, who was a member of a prominent Cumbrian family residing in the Penrith area.[24] The book contains an elaborate and witnessed account of his gift of the manuscript to his wife's sister-in-law, Jane Burdett, wife of Sir Thomas Burdett, first baronet (d.1647). She forthwith bequeathed it to her son, Frauncys, the second baronet (d.1696), to be an heirloom in his family 'whilst God Continues your name or Blood in posteritie'.[25] The volume duly remained in the possession of the Burdett family until only very recently.[26]

In this remarkably well-documented history, only the personal identity of the original owner (and presumably patron) of this exceptionally beautiful psalter-hours remains obscure. He is represented in one full-page miniature (Fig. 1) and alongside four of the historiated initials (Figs 7, 11, 12, and 13), in every case wearing the distinctive dress of a Hospitaller, but is more precisely identified by no clues at all, either personal or textual. There is no question but that the manuscript was decorated in France, its illuminator being located in Paris. It has been suggested by François Avril that the most likely candidate for patron is Jean de Villiers, who was French Grand Prior of the order from 1282 to 1285 and Grand Master of the entire Order between 1285 and 1293. Having served in the east during the earlier part of his career, he apparently came back to Paris in 1282, remaining in France until the summer of 1286. He then returned to the Holy Land for the final period of Latin occupation and was among the leaders of the defendants of the doomed city of Acre, which fell to the forces of Islam on 18 May 1291. Jean de Villiers was one of the few Knights Hospitaller who escaped alive from the terrible carnage of that day. The order removed to Limasol in Cyprus and there he seems to have remained until his death, which apparently took place in 1294. These dates certainly accord quite satisfactorily with other evidence concerning the

[24]   T. H. B. Graham, 'The Huttons of Cumberland', *Transactions of the Cumberland and Westmorland Antiquarian and Archaeological Society*, n.s., 30, 1930, pp. 68–88.

[25]   For the connection between the two families see G. Watson, 'The Burdetts of Bramcote and the Huttons of Penrith', *Transactions of the Cumberland and Westmorland Antiquarian and Archaeological Society*, n.s., 3, 1903, pp. 269–71.

[26]   The bookplate of the fifth baronet, Sir Francis Burdett (1770–1844) is in the manuscript. A note records that it later belonged to the seventh and eighth baronets. It remained with the family until it was sold by private treaty in 1990.

history of the manuscript, though they do not provide any obvious explanation for the circumstances of its migration to England so early in its history.[27]

However, the distinctly English symptoms within the manuscript's original textual content surely suggest that the patron could have been an Englishman. In England, as in France, senior members of the order were very highly ranked. One late thirteenth-century Grand Prior of the Hospitallers, Joseph de Chauncy (1273–80), was at the same time treasurer to Edward I, whose attention he had attracted when both were serving in the east before Edward's accession. He was apparently a member of a well-known family with lands in Yorkshire and Lincolnshire,[28] had been general treasurer of the Order since 1248 and probably resumed this position on return to the Holy Land in 1280.[29] He has some claim to be a patron of the arts, being responsible for major building work at the Order's headquarters in Clerkenwell during his time as Grand Prior.[30] His successor, William de Henley (1281–90), built the Clerkenwell cloisters.[31] He too in due course returned to the Holy Land, leaving England in the summer of 1290 and losing his life at Acre in the following year.[32] The next two Grand Priors, Peter de Hakehan (1290–97) and William de Tothale (1297–1315), seem to have been more firmly rooted in England. Both are frequently mentioned in the patent rolls as appointing attorneys, the former on account of his ill-health, the latter because of his heavy administrative burdens which embraced Scotland and Wales as well as England.[33] Throughout the relevant period there was of course constant movement between England and France, not merely in the general course of travel but specifically because of Edward I's political and territorial interests.[34] Detailed information about the activities and interests of the Hospitallers at the time is not easy to extract. Their history and organisation are far better served for the fourteenth century, when extensive property surveys were drawn up in the wake of the suppression of the Templars in 1312, much of

27   Christopher de Hamel has constructed a most lively history for the book in his Sotheby's sale catalogue for 23 June 1998. It is however based solely on the assumption that Jean de Villiers really did own the psalter hours.

28   Several members of the family are detailed in Moor 1929–32 (as n. 18 above), vol. 1, pp. 196–8.

29   M. Prestwich, *Edward I*, London 1988, pp. 81, 234.

30   H. W. Fincham, *The Order of the Hospital of St John of Jerusalem and its Grand Priory of England*, London 1933, p. 73.

31   Ibid.

32   E. King and H. Luke, *The Knights of St John in the British Realm*, London 1967, pp. 31–2.

33   In each year between 1293 and 1301 attorneys were appointed, see *Calendar of Patent Rolls: Edward I, 1292–1301*, London 1895, pp. 16, 75, 138, 194, 256, 312, 336, 358, 400, 492 and 581.

34   See Prestwich 1988 (as n. 29 above), especially chs. 11 and 12.

their landed endowment passing to the Hospital.[35]

The costume worn by the manuscript's patron does not necessarily identify him as a high-ranking member of the Order, however. This seems to be the earliest surviving image of a Hospitaller. Medieval and Renaissance depictions in general suggest that there were no great variations in the standard dress of a black mantle over a black or dark-coloured gown, with the eight-pointed white cross, later known as the Cross of Malta, usually on the shoulder of the former garment. In an early sixteenth-century gospel lectionary in the British Library, Grand Master Philippe Villiers de l'Isle Adam is seen in a rich, fur-lined contemporary version of this costume, kneeling, like the owner of the psalter-hours, at the feet of the Baptist in his role as patron of the order.[36] Hospitallers are included among the sequence of members of the religious orders in the margins of the early fifteenth-century Sherborne Missal, identified by their black mantles charged with a white cross, the garments shown as lined with vair.[37] Very slightly earlier, several images of Juan Fernandez de Heredia, the highly distinguished Aragonese Master of Rhodes (d. 1396), show a similar costume, the hood of the mantle raised over his head.[38] The distinctive little round, tasselled hat worn by the patron of the psalter-hours is exactly paralleled in an image of three Hospitallers in attendance upon Pope Benedict XI in the fourteenth-century *Liber Indulgentiae*[39] and thus apparently has no special significance. The patron could in fact be any member of the Order whose family circumstances were such as to permit the commissioning of so elaborate a book.

Support for and interest in the Crusades persisted in England as the Latin grip on the Holy Land loosened. The king himself took the cross for a second time in 1287.[40] There are various references of relevance in the biographical records of several of the persons associated with the 'Very Old Book'. Robert de Vere, Earl of Oxford, is said to have been a patron of the Hospitallers.[41] Denise de Munchensy's son William, father of the younger Denise, willed 900 marks, a very substantial sum, for the good of the Holy Land.[42] His cousin William, great-grandson of Margery de Crek, having apparently conspired to murder, was sentenced in 1286 to go to the Holy Land within a year and

35   See M. Gervers, *The Hospitaller Cartulary in the British Library (Cotton MS Nero E. vi): A Study of the Manuscript and its Composition*, Toronto 1982, and idem. *The Cartulary of the Knights of St John of Jerusalem in England: Seconda Camera, Essex*, London 1982.
36   London, British Lib. MS Add. 18143, fol. 4r.
37   London, British Lib. MS Add. 74326, p. 371 (lower margin).
38   Reproduced in H. J. A. Sire, *The Knights of Malta*, New Haven and London 1994, colour plate IV, and pp. 42, 43.
39   Ibid., p. 41.
40   Prestwich 1988 (as n. 29 above), p. 328.
41   Cockayne 1910–59 (as n. 13 above), vol. 10, p. 217.
42   Moor 1929–32 (as n. 18 above), vol. 3, pp. 178–9.

remain there in God's service forever. It seems that he did not comply for nearly a decade, but 100 marks from his lands were payable to the Prior of the Hospitallers, in England or in Acre, in February 1291.[43] There are also possible territorial links. The Hospitallers were firmly established in eastern England, with a preceptory of central importance at Chippenham in Cambridgeshire, not far distant from Waterbeach. In the 1290s it was headed by Nicolas de Accombe, a leading figure in the Order who appears several times among the attorneys named by both Peter de Hakeham and William de Tothale.[44]

More definite information may in due course emerge to place the Burdett family's Hospitaller manuscript in context. Its central importance lies in the fact that, like the Solger Hours in Nuremberg and the Murthly Hours in the National Library of Scotland, it is a French-made manuscript of the very first quality that can be placed quite firmly in England at the end of the thirteenth century, introducing the styles of the Parisian workshops into those English circles most likely to commission substantial illuminated books on this side of the Channel.

[43]   Ibid., p. 179. See also Cockayne 1910–59 (as n. 13 above), vol. 9, p. 416.
[44]   See n. 33 above. For Chippenham see Victoria County History, *Cambridgeshire*, vol. 2, London 1967, pp. 264–6. It is worth noting that one Henry de Acom, 'chafewax' in Chancery, is concerned with land transactions also involving the Hutton family in and around 1327, see Graham 1930 (as n. 24 above).

The Saunders Lecture 1997

The Images of Words in English Gothic Psalters

LUCY FREEMAN SANDLER

Both the 1996 exhibition, 'Het Utrechts Psalter. Middeleeuwse meesterwerken rond een beroemd handschrift', and the accompanying catalogue, *The Utrecht Psalter in Medieval Art. Picturing the Psalms of David,* focused attention on a number of interesting questions about the making of manuscripts – among them, of course, the nature of copying, but also the relation between text and image and, above all, the meaning of the term 'literal illustration'.[1] Consideration of these questions in relation to the Utrecht Psalter and its derivatives has led me to think that raising them in connection with psalters executed in England later than the last known descendant of the Carolingian model might be productive.

The continued viability of the literal mode of psalter illustration into the thirteenth and fourteenth centuries is demonstrated in a number of English books with historiated initials for every psalm, and also in some famous English psalters that have marginal images on every text page. These manuscripts include the Paris Psalter, the last derivative of the Utrecht Psalter, produced in Canterbury around 1190,[2] the Cuerden Psalter in the Pierpont Morgan Library in New York, perhaps made in Oxford around 1270,[3] the De la Twyere Psalter at the New York Public Library, made for use in York diocese during the first decade of the fourteenth century,[4] and the

---

[1] *The Utrecht Psalter in Medieval Art, Picturing the Psalms of David*, K. van der Horst, W. Noel, and W. C. M. Wüstefeld (eds), MS't Goy 1996, in conjunction with the exhibition titled 'Het Utrechts Psalter. Middeleeuwse meesterwerken rond een beroemd handschrift', Utrecht, Catharijneconvent, 31 August–17 November 1996.

[2] Paris, Bibl. nationale MS lat. 8846; see *Utrecht Psalter* 1996 (as n.1 above), no. 30.

[3] New York, Pierpont Morgan Lib. MS M.756; see N. J. Morgan, *Early Gothic Manuscripts [II], 1250–1285* (A Survey of Manuscripts Illuminated in the British Isles, J. J. G. Alexander [ed.], vol. 4, 2), London 1988, no. 162.

[4] New York, Public Lib. MS Spencer 2; see L. F. Sandler, *Gothic Manuscripts 1285–1385* (A Survey of Manuscripts Illuminated in the British Isles, J. J. G. Alexander [ed.], vol. 5), London 1986, vol. 2, no. 36.

psalter in Vienna started for Humphrey de Bohun perhaps around 1350[5] (all with historiated psalm initials), as well as the Gorleston Psalter in the British Library, made for use in East Anglia round 1310-1320,[6] and the Luttrell Psalter, made for Geoffrey Luttrell of Lincolnshire around 1325-1335,[7] (both of these with marginal illustrations on every page).[8]

The term 'literal illustration' is inadequate as a description of the complexities of relationship between text and image in these manuscripts. Its implied certainty that pictures are exact translations of words seems too simple. Consequently, in the title of this essay I have replaced 'literal illustration' with 'images of words', in the hope that this phrase will suggest a somewhat broader range of relationships than the kind of subservience of image to text evoked by the pairing of 'literal' and 'illustration'. But whether we use 'literal illustration' or 'word imagery' we may ask in the first place why either phrase is used consistently and almost solely in connection with a pictorial mode employed in medieval psalters. Should not all manuscript illustrations that correspond closely with a text be termed 'literal'? Taking the biblical narrative of Cain and Abel as an example, in the Authorized Version of Genesis (4.8-9) we read that 'Cain rose up against Abel his brother, and slew him. And the Lord said unto Cain, Where is Abel thy brother? And he said, I know not: Am I my brother's keeper?' In the modern American *Good News Bible*,[9] however, the corresponding passage reads: 'Cain turned on his brother and killed him. The Lord asked Cain, Where is your brother Abel? He answered, I don't know. Am I supposed to take care of my brother?' In a sense the verbal difference does not matter, except to our literary sensibilities. Whether one translation or the other, the text is a narrative that can be given a narrative pictorial form despite the different

---

[5]   Vienna, Österreichische Nationalbibl. cod. 1826*; see Sandler 1986 (as n. 4 above), vol. 2, no. 133, with further bibliography. Present opinion tends to attribute the original patronage of the manuscript to Humphrey de Bohun, 6th Earl of Hereford, d. 1361, and posits a date as early as 1348 for the beginning of work on the book; see L. Dennison, '"The Fitzwarin Psalter and its Allies": A Reappraisal', in *England in the Fourteenth Century*, W. M. Ormrod (ed.), Woodbridge, Suffolk 1986, pp. 42-66.

[6]   London, British Lib. MS Add. 49622; see Sandler 1986 (as n. 4 above), vol. 2, no. 50. S. C. Cockerell, *The Gorleston Psalter*, London 1907, had dated the Gorleston Psalter before 1306; see, most recently, J. Goodall, 'Heraldry in the Decoration of English Medieval Manuscripts', *Antiquaries Journal* 78, 1997, pp.185-6.

[7]   London, British Lib. MS Add. 42130; see *The Luttrell Psalter*, E. G. Millar, London 1932, dating the Luttrell Psalter c.1340-45, and Sandler 1986 (as n. 4 above), vol. 2, no. 107.

[8]   The marginalia of the Luttrell Psalter ends at Psalm 118 (fol. 215).

[9]   *Good News Bible: The Bible in Today's English Version* (published by the American Bible Society), New York 1966-76.

words, and indeed all biblical illustrations of the murder of Abel would be expected to have the same action and actors.

But the psalms, despite their vivid, evocative, and dramatic verbal imagery, are not narrative. 'Direct' illustration of the text produces not narrative but word images. As Adelheid Heimann observed, and William Noel has recalled,[10] recourse to the three differing versions of the psalms in the Utrecht Psalter and its relations is sometimes accountable for different pictorial components in the illustrations. So, for instance, the Gallican text of the Utrecht Psalter Psalm 27.7, 'The Lord is my helper and my protector', corresponds with the pictorial motif of the Lord commanding an angel holding an umbrella over the figure of the psalmist,[11] and this image is repeated in the Eadwine Psalter, which has the texts of the Roman and Hebrew as well as the Gallican version;[12] on the other hand, the Paris Psalter, which also has all three versions, has an illustration for Psalm 27.7 that corresponds with the *Hebraica*, 'The Lord is my strength and my shield', in showing the angel with a shield rather than an umbrella.[13] In sum, these illustrations differ because the words themselves 'count' in a way that they do not in illustrations of the biblical narrative about Cain and Abel.

How words count in English Gothic psalter illustration is the subject of the essay that follows. I have four aims: first to define literal illustration in as multifaceted a way as possible, an effort that will gain breadth from the inclusion of thirteenth- and fourteenth-century psalters unrelated in format to those of the Utrecht group; second, to discuss the various physical relationships between text and word images, that is, how the format in which the word images are presented affects the choice and subjects of the illustrations; third, to address the question of literal illustration as a tradition, to judge the degree of continuity and evaluate the means by which continuity was sustained; and finally, to speculate about the impact of literal illustration

[10]   *Utrecht Psalter* 1996 (as n. 1 above), p. 134, citing A. Heimann, 'The Last Copy of the Utrecht Psalter', in *The Year 1200. A Symposium*, New York 1975, p. 315; see also D. Panofsky, 'The Textual Basis of the Utrecht Psalter Illustrations', *Art Bulletin* 25, 1943, pp. 50–8, citing a number of instances of recourse to the *Hebraica* version of the Psalms, and Koert van der Horst's rebuttal in *Utrecht Psalter* 1996 (as n. 1 above), pp. 72–3.

[11]   Utrecht, University Lib. MS 32, Hautvilliers (Reims), *c.*820–35. See *Utrecht Psalter. Vollständige Faksimile-Ausgabe im Originalformat der Handschrift 32 aus dem Besitz der Bibliothek der Rijksuniversiteit Utrecht* (Codices selecti, 75), K. van der Horst and J. H. A. Engelbregt (eds), Graz 1984.

[12]   Cambridge, Trinity Coll. MS R.17.1, Canterbury, Christ Church *c.*1155–60; see *The Canterbury Psalter*, M. R. James (ed.), London 1935, fol. 46v (facsimile).

[13]   Canterbury, Christ Church, *c.*1180–1200, and Catalonia, *c.*1350; see *Psautier illustré (XIIIe S.). Reproduction des 107 miniatures du manuscrit latin 8846 de la Bibliothèque nationale*, H. Omont (ed.), Paris 1906, pl. 36.

on looking, reading, and remembering – in short, on the use of the book to its possessor.

The simplest literal illustrations of the psalms single out individual concrete nouns, or pronouns, and present their visual equivalents. Words for human beings are pictured in accordance with gender and status, and given some attribute to identify them. Enemies and the wicked are armed men; the just and righteous carry books or palm branches; fools carry baubles; kings are bearded and crowned figures. The 'I' of the psalms may also be shown as crowned, playing a harp, clearly David. God, made visible of course, has a cruciform halo, and is usually in the upper part of the image, often associated with common Christian symbols (clouds, mandorla, angels). Other *invisibilia* are also given visible form, for instance the soul, either as a bird, or as a small, naked figure. In his essay in the Utrecht Psalter exhibition catalogue Koert van der Horst called such frequently repeated word-images 'formulaic'.[14]

However, many concrete nouns in the psalms are used figuratively or metaphorically. For example, in Psalm 8.8–9, David praises God, saying 'Thou has subjected all things under his [i.e., man's] feet, all sheep and oxen; moreover the beasts also of the fields. The birds of the air, and the fishes of the sea'.[15] The creatures and the natural elements named are depicted *ad verbum* in the illustration in the Paris Psalter (Fig. 1). Yet if we read Psalm 22.1–2 however, we find comparable nouns used figuratively: 'The lord ruleth me: and I shall want nothing. He hath set me in a place of pasture. He hath brought me up, on the water of refreshment'. In the Paris Psalter illustration of this passage (Fig. 2), the images are direct equivalents of the verbal metaphors.

Direct pictorial equivalents of nouns used figuratively in the psalms often produce images that are striking and memorable. Psalm 44.2, 'My tongue is the pen of a scrivener', in both the Paris Psalter[16] and the Cuerden Psalter (Fig. 3) is illustrated with a writer, in the Cuerden Psalter, David himself. In the Twyere Psalter, Psalm 8.3, 'Out of the mouths of infants and sucklings thou hast perfected praise' (Fig. 4), and Psalm 22.4, 'Thy rod and thy staff ['virga' and 'baculus'] they have comforted me' (Fig. 5), are both illustrated with noun-equivalents, the first with a pair of infants in arms, one nursing at the breast of its mother, and the other, with a boy holding a brushy rod. Similarly, Psalm 10, 'How then do you say then to my soul: Get thee away from hence to the mountain like a sparrow?' is represented in the Bohun Psalter by a sparrow flying away from a deathly pale reclining male figure and toward a mountain (Fig. 6).

The actions of some verbs in the psalms are also transposed into equivalent pictorial actions, usually carrying along their noun subjects or

14   *Utrecht Psalter* 1996 (as n. 1 above), pp. 64–5.
15   All psalm texts from the Douay-Rheims version.
16   Paris Psalter, fol. 79v; see *Psautier illustré* 1906 (as n. 13 above), pl. 53.

objects. Examples abound among the musical verbs that are so frequent in the psalms: Psalm 32 for example, which begins, 'Rejoice in the Lord, O ye just: praise becometh the upright. Give praise to the Lord on the harp; sing to him with the psaltery, the instrument of ten strings. Sing to him a new canticle', is illustrated with figures playing stringed instruments in the Paris Psalter, the Cuerden Psalter and the Bohun Psalter.[17] 'Cantate domino canticum novum' begins Psalm 97, and singing figures appear in countless historiated initials for this psalm, including those of psalters not otherwise illustrated throughout *ad verbum*.[18] Other verbs represented directly reflect various emotional or prayerful states: 'Upon the rivers of Babylon we sat and wept' (Psalm 136.1) is coupled in the Gorleston Psalter with a grieving woman and man in the upper margin, directly above the relevant words 'sedimus' and 'flevimus'.[19] In the Twyere Psalter, Psalm 142.1, 'Hear, O Lord my prayer: Give ear to my supplication', corresponds with the historiation of the initial, showing the naked soul of a man (142.3, 'For the enemy hath persecuted my soul: he hath brought down my life to earth') in prayer before the Lord, who blesses the supplicant (Fig. 7).

But verbs, like nouns, are often used metaphorically in the psalms. When verbal metaphors are turned directly into images, the result may parallel the meaning of the text, elucidate it, amplify it, dramatise it or even negate it. Psalm 25 in the Paris Psalter may serve as an example (Fig. 8): verses 5 and 6, 'I have hated the assembly of the malignant; and with the wicked I will not sit. I will wash my hands among the innocent', elicited a pair of white-garbed men, the innocents, washing their hands in a central basin, an image that suits the action to the words. The terse phrasing of verse 6, 'I will wash my hands among the innocent' is translated visually in expanded form, since it is not the psalmist who is washing his hands but the innocents; as if the verse were expanded to read 'I will wash my hands among the innocent who wash their hands', and the psalmist stands adjacent, a scroll in one hand and the other palm up in a gesture of avowal, representing the words, 'I will'.

Among other examples of this kind of pictorial acting out consonant with text words and phrases are Psalm 78.1 in the Cuerden Psalter, 'O God, the heathens are come into thy inheritance, they have defiled thy holy temple', with a pair of men literally painting dirty streaks on the walls of the temple of the Lord (Fig. 9); Psalm 125.5-7 in the Bohun Psalter, 'They that sow in tears shall reap in joy. Going they went and wept, casting their seeds. But coming,

---

17   Paris Psalter, fol. 54v; Cuerden Psalter, fol. 48; Bohun Psalter, fol. 30v.

18   Historiated initials for Psalm 97, the first of the psalms recited at Matins on Saturday, mark the beginning of one of the eight divisions of the liturgical psalter. The standard historiated initial shows clerics chanting at a lectern. In addition, in both the Gorleston Psalter (fol. 126) and the Luttrell Psalter (fol. 174v, Ps. 97. 3–8), musicians appear in the margins.

19   Gorleston Psalter, fol. 177.

they shall come with joyfulness, carrying their sheaves', with a scene of sowing little white seeds on either side of the initial letter 'I' (Fig. 10); and Psalm 93.6 in the Luttrell Psalter, 'They have slain the widow and the stranger: and they have murdered the fatherless', with three vignettes of murder (Fig. 11), a motif repeated in the Bohun Psalter.[20]

Sometimes, however, the action is depicted 'out of context' to a lesser or greater degree, consequently altering the parallel between text and image. To return to the Paris Psalter illustration of Psalm 25 (Fig. 8), the psalmist in the foreground stands on a base from which flames are shooting upward. This motif is the pictorial equivalent of verse 2, 'Prove me, O Lord, and try me; burn my reins and my heart'. In this case direct pictorial translation of a figure of speech results in a powerful, but somewhat cryptic image that demands recourse to, or recall of, the text for explanation.

Still more stimulating to an active involvement of the reader with the text are those images that act out verbs in a thoroughly decontextualised way. The chief examples occur in marginal illustrations, where it is not uncommon to find that the verbal action is carried out by some outré creature, as, for instance, in the Luttrell Psalter, Psalm 34.13, where below the last line on the page, 'But as for me, when they were troublesome to me', is a man threatened by a devilish creature armed with a gold tipped spear (Fig. 12). The 'they' who 'were troublesome to me' are the psalmist's enemies, who have 'repaid me evil for good' so the aggressor is also a dramatically heightened visualisation of David's strong feelings of being beleaguered.

The verb *probare* mentioned in connection with the illustration of Psalm 25 in the Paris Psalter is associated in more than one case with proof or trial by fire in psalm imagery. For example, Psalm 16.3, 'Thou has proved my heart, and visited it by night thou hast tried me by fire: and iniquity hath not been found in me' corresponds in the Cuerden psalter to a praying man engulfed in flames (Fig. 13); this is turned into a pictorial example in the Twyere Psalter by representing the tortured figure as St Lawrence lying on a grill above a roaring fire tended by two men, one with a pair of bellows.[21] The Twyere image follows a common pattern, in which the situation or actions described by the words is explicated by a visual example.[22]

Again, the examples may be consonant in spirit with the words of the psalms, or they may diverge in various degrees. Sometimes the artist

[20] Bohun Psalter, fol. 82v, showing two men attacking two women, one of about thirty illustrations in the manuscript that are based on passages beyond the opening lines of the psalm.
[21] Twyere Psalter, fol. 31.
[22] For example, in psalters with historiated initials at the liturgical divisions of the text, Psalm 68.2, 'Save me, O God: for the waters are come in even unto my soul' was frequently illustrated with an Old Testament example of Jonah and the Whale.

developed the pictorial example from a word or phrase that is quite non-specific, for instance, the opening of Psalm 11, 'Save me, O Lord, for there is now no saint'. In the Cuerden Psalter this line corresponds to the image of the Lord rescuing a man from a fiery pit (Fig. 14); in the Bohun Psalter the Lord is saving David from drowning, a motif undoubtedly inspired by the common illustration for Psalm 68, 'Save me, O God: for the waters are come in even unto my soul'.[23]

Some pictorial examples are related to common literary exempla of the sort employed in Christian exegesis, or to visual images familiar from other contexts, and thus readily identifiable with the words or phrases of the psalms to which they pertain. In the Bohun Psalter, for instance, Psalm 132.1, 'Behold how good and how pleasant it is for brethren to dwell together in unity', is illustrated with a pair of men embracing, emblematic of brotherly love,[24] and Psalm 36.1, 'Be not emulous of evildoers', with a man virtuously turning away from a man and woman kissing, the concept of evildoing exemplified by an act of lust (Fig. 15).

The pictorial examples may be familiar religious subjects. Considering the violence and suffering that is such a concern of the psalter text it is not surprising that images that exemplify phrases such as 'Whilst the wicked draw near against me to eat my flesh', or 'My enemies that trouble me' or 'If a battle should rise up against me', all on the Psalm 26 page of the Luttrell Psalter, should elicit a vignette of the martyrdom of St Thomas of Canterbury in the bottom margin (Fig. 16).

Some visual examples are clearly typological. In the Paris Psalter Psalm 21, which begins, 'O God my God, look upon me: why hast thou forsaken me', and includes the line, 'they parted my garments amongst them; and upon my vesture they cast lots', calls forth a cross hung with the instruments of Christ's passion.[25] In the Luttrell Psalter the initial of Psalm 44,[26] which in Christian exegesis celebrates the marriage of Christ and the Church, shows the Virgin and Child, and on the same page, below the words of Psalm 44.3, 'Thou art beautiful above the sons of men: grace is poured abroad in thy lips', is the Annunciation, the blank scroll of the angel readily filled in the viewer's mind with the words of the angelic salutation, 'Hail, full of grace' (Luke 1.28).

Pictorial examples of words or phrases in the psalms are not, however, always so readily recognisable. They sometimes demand an active engagement

---

[23]   As, for example, in the historiated initial for Psalm 68 in the Luttrell Psalter (fol. 121v).

[24]   Cf. the English encyclopaedia of 1360–75, *Omne bonum* (London, British Lib. MS Royal 6 B vi, fol. 85v), in which the entry for *Amicicia* shows two men embracing; see L. F. Sandler, *Omne bonum, A Fourteenth-century Encyclopedia of Universal Knowledge*, vol. 2, London 1996, p. 37.

[25]   Paris Psalter, fol. 36v; see *Psautier illustré* 1906 (as n. 13 above), pl. 30.

[26]   Luttrell Psalter, fol. 86; see *Luttrell Psalter* 1932 (as n. 7 above), pl. 27d.

with the text before they yield their relevance, and I believe, as I will elaborate further below, that this kind of dynamic text-image relationship was envisioned in the Middle Ages too. Such examples are characteristic of psalters with marginal illustrations, especially the Luttrell Psalter. For instance, Psalm 88.20–21, 'Then thou [i.e., the Lord] has spoken in a vision to thy saints, and saidst: I have laid help upon one that is mighty, and have exalted one chosen out of my people. I have found David my servant: with my holy oil I have anointed him', is illustrated directly in the Anglo-Saxon Bury Psalter in the Vatican Library with a marginal vignette of the anointing of David.[27] But in the Luttrell Psalter the words are associated with the unction of an ordinary dying man, not the royal David. Omitting a pictorial reference to David, the marginal image shows Christ, attended by an angel, anointing the forehead of the moribund penitent (Fig. 17). In this way, the promise of the Lord to his saints, that he would exalt an elect of his people, that with his holy oil he would anoint him, is applied visually to all people (including the user of this manuscript) offering believers in Christ a vision of beatitude at the end of life.

Some of the numerous genre subjects in the Luttrell Psalter are also pictorial examples based on text passages. One of the nicest cases is the extended cycle of images of food preparation that begins below Psalm 113.4, where the words, 'the works of the hands of men' are found (Fig. 18).[28] Here, however, 'based on text passages' refers to an image developed by taking the words out of context, so that the illustration exemplifies the 'works of the hands of men' in a manner quite different from the way this phrase is used in the psalm, where, in fact, we read 'The idols of the Gentiles are silver and gold, the works of the hands of men'. What lesson was to be drawn from this decontextualisation of the image, and, indeed, from its disregard of the spirit of the text? It may be that here the manuscript user was being offered a 'better' visual example of the works of men than the making of idols, and this explanation is perhaps justified by the fact that the culminating marginal vignette of the series shows the consumption of the meal by the members of the Luttrell family, the original commissioners of the manuscript. Undoubtedly, in their eyes, the labour that put food on their table was worthy in the sight of God.

The disengagement of word-images from their contexts is linked with the invention of complex images of two kinds found only in Gothic psalters with marginal illustrations. The first is the type of vignette in which the image of a

[27] Bury Psalter, early eleventh century (Bibl. Apostolica Vaticana MS Reg. lat. 12), fol. 95; see *Anglo-Saxon Textual Illustration: Photographs of Sixteen Manuscripts with Descriptions and Index*, T. H. Ohlgren, (ed.), Kalamazoo 1992, pl. 3.38.

[28] The series consists of four images (fols 206v – 208); cf. M. Camille, 'Labouring for the Lord: The Ploughman and the Social Order in the Luttrell Psalter', *Art History* 10, 1987, pp. 423–54 (esp. pp. 439–41, commenting on another case of word imagery in the same cycle).

single word is one element in a complex image unrelated as a whole to the text; the second is the type of complex but unitary image that incorporates word equivalents from a variety of places in a particular psalm, again without representing in any way the grammatical structure or meaning of those passages from which the visual motifs were extracted. The Luttrell Psalter provides the best examples.[29] The strategy that produced the first type, that is, a non-contextual image with a single verbal tie to the text, often resulted in grotesques, for example, on the page with Psalm 105. 41–42, 'And he [the Lord] delivered them into the hands of the nations: and they that hated them had dominion over them. And their enemies afflicted them: and they were humbled under their hands'.[30] Paralleling these lines is a marginal monster whose hands are where his feet would be. The incongruous components, of course, are what makes the creature monstrous, but among them the hands stand out particularly, not only because of their position in the body but because of their inversion in relation to the profile of the other components of the figure. Such monsters may evoke generally the threatening forces named in the psalms: the unjust, the iniquitous, the enemies that harry, oppress and terrify the psalmist, although by no means is there psalm-by-psalm correlation between marginal monsters and the tenor of the text.

The second type of non-contextual marginalia, the kind developed by combining pictorial equivalents of disparate words on a particular page, is found in some astounding images in the Luttrell Psalter. One is a kind of Eleanor cross held aloft by a giant man balancing on one foot; at its base sits a small figure, hand raised to brow in a gesture of wonderment; near the top of the cross are three crowned effigies of Eleanor, and just below the pennant at its summit is the cross proper, that is, a crucified Christ.[31] Adjacent to this image are the lines of Psalm 88.7–9, 'For who in the clouds can be compared to the Lord or who among the sons of God shall be like to God: God who is glorified in the assembly of the saints: great and terrible above them all that are about him. O Lord God of hosts,who is like to thee?'[32] Metaphorically, the stone cross base is raised up in the clouds and God, that is, the crucified Christ, is glorified above all them, the female figures, that are about him. God is great and terrible, hence the seated man's gesture of wonder. The idea of representing such a freestanding polygonal structure may have come from the

---

[29] See L. F. Sandler, 'The Word in the Text and the Image in the Margin: The Case of the Luttrell Psalter', *Journal of the Walters Art Gallery* 54, 1996, pp. 87–100.

[30] Luttrell Psalter, fol. 193v; *Luttrell Psalter* 1932 (as n. 7 above), pl. 139.

[31] Luttrell Psalter, fol. 159v; *Luttrell Psalter* 1932 (as n. 7 above), pl. 71.

[32] Psalm 88. 7–9: 'Quoniam quis *in nubibus* equabitur *domino*: similis erit domino in filiis dei. *Deus qui glorificatur* in consilio sanctorum: *magnus and terribilis super omnes qui in circuitu eius sunt.* Domine deus virtutum quis similis tibi: *potens* es domine and veritas tua *in circuitu tuo*" (pictorial word-equivalents italicised).

twice-repeated term 'in circuitu', and the strongman holding the structure up is literally 'potens'.

In this image all the words are gathered together in a single non-contextual entity. Word-images may also constitute a mock narrative, as in the Luttrell Psalter illustration for Psalm 88.12–15, which runs down the whole length of the page.[33] The pictorial action is plausible, four men straining to row a boat pulled by two more; but what in the text could have elicited the image? Again we find the verbal sources in key words scattered in the adjacent lines of the psalm text: 'Thine are the heavens and thine is the earth: the world and the fullness thereof thou has founded: the north and the sea thou hast created. Thabor and Hermon shall rejoice in thy name: thy arm is with might. Let thy hand be strengthened and the right hand exalted: justice and judgment are the preparation of thy throne. Mercy and truth shall go before thy face'.[34] The key words, 'mare', 'brachium cum potencia', 'firmetur manus tua', 'sedis tua' and 'precedent faciem tuam' can be combined into a new sentence that would parallel the features of the marginal image. It would read something like this: 'With their strong hands they go before the faces of men seated in a boat rowed through the sea by the power of their arms'.

The most extreme form of decontextualisation is the pictorial image that corresponds not to a word or phrase but to a single syllable, a mode again prevalent in marginal illustrations of psalters. Michael Camille has called attention to the medieval fascination with scriptural words whose syllables are common vernacular terms for parts of the body associated with sex and defaecation: *vit* from *vita*, or *cul* from *iuvencularum* or *conculcavit*.[35] This fascination is reflected in the Gorleston Psalter, for example, on the page with Psalm 44.10, 'The queen stood on thy right hand' on the second line.[36] The 'As' of 'Astitit' at the beginning of the line may have elicited the obscene arse-end view of the man in the upper margin, directly above the first two letters of the word,[37] while the crowned female hybrid in the lower margin

[33] Luttrell Psalter, fol. 160; *Luttrell Psalter* 1932 (as n. 7 above), pl. 72.
[34] Psalm 88. 12–15: 'Tui sunt celi and tua est terra: orbem terre and plenitudinem eius tu fundasti: aquilonem and *mare* tu creasti. Thabor and hermon in nomine tuo exultabunt: *tuum brachium cum potencia. Firmetur manus tua and exaltetur dextera tua: iusticia and iudicium preparacio* sedis tue. Misericordia and veritas *precedent faciem tuam*' (pictorial word-equivalents italicised).
[35] M. Camille, *Image on the Edge, The Margins of Medieval Art*, London 1992, pp. 39, 43.
[36] Psalm 44.10: 'Astitit regina a dextris tuis in vestitu deaurato circumdita varietate'.
[37] This is not the only marginal instance of trans-linguistic pictorial-syllabic play. See Camille 1992 (as n. 35 above), p. 43 and figs 21–2 associating the *cul* (Anglo-French) of *iuvencularum* (Latin) with the exposed backside of a nude in the bottom margin or a page from the thirteenth-century Rutland Psalter (London, British Lib. MS Add. 62925, fol. 67) with the words of Psalm 67.26 in the last line; see *The Rutland Psalter*, E. G. Millar (ed.), Oxford 1937 (facsimile).

responds to the next word, 'regina'. Other syllabic images are less earthy, as for instance, the treatment of Psalm 83.2–3, 'My heart and my flesh have rejoiced in the living God. For the sparrow hath found herself a house', etc. In the Twyere Psalter illustration of this psalm the word 'sparrow' is transposed directly (Fig. 19); but in the Luttrell Psalter the word 'passer', in the last line of the page, has been syllabified pictorially (Fig. 20). 'Pas' is now translated into a pictorial action of two naked men[38] 'pes', or 'foot', to foot. As astounding as the 'footsie' image is, it may well have had recognition value in the Middle Ages, since comparable images, not elicited by textual passages, occur in the margins of the Rutland Psalter and elsewhere.[39] Just as in the game of charades, where the player is challenged to identify a word, or a phrase, unless he or she comprehends the action that represents it, the task is hopeless.

To sum up, word images are not all alike in the ways they are related to the text. Some are direct pictorial equivalents that correspond to the sense of the psalm; some are transpositions of words and phrases that are already metaphorical into direct pictorial equivalents, in the process altering the way the text is looked at; some 'illustrate' words and phrases with visual examples; and some are so decontextualised that they appear to disregard the sense of the text completely.

The second part of this essay considers how the types of transposition of words into images and the resulting word-images themselves intersect with the physical format of the psalter, whether it is a question of the full-width miniatures of the Paris Psalter, the historiated initials of such books as the Bohun Psalter, or the marginalia of the Luttrell Psalter. Ancient layouts of book illustration, evident in the Utrecht Psalter, clearly persist in the Paris Psalter: first, the pictures are physically *in* the text; they are exactly the width of the text block, like the illustrations of other works of great antiquity such as the Vatican Vergil.[40] Second, the images are collective, that is, they pull

---

For another instance from the Rutland Psalter, see below. Some of Camille's finds are not convincing, as, for example, his identification (p. 39, fig. 17) of a 'phallic turban' as the pictorial equivalent of *conturbata* (Psalm 6.3) on the Penitential Psalms page of the Grey-Fitzpayn Hours (Cambridge, Fitzwilliam Mus. MS 242, fol. 55v). *Turbata* did not occur in English or French with the present meaning before the sixteenth century; with the spelling *tuliban, tollipane*, etc. the word occurs in French as early as the fifteenth century; see *Oxford English Dictionary*, 2nd. ed., Oxford 1989 and *Dictionnaire historique de la langue française*, Paris 1992, s.v.

[38] Their nakedness apparently responds to the phrase 'My heart and my flesh' (Cor meum and *caro mea*) of verse 2, at the beginning of the third line from the bottom of the page. In the Rutland Psalter parallel cited in note 39 below the foot wrestlers are clothed.

[39] Rutland Psalter, London, British Lib. MS Add. 62925, fol. 43v; *Rutland Psalter* 1937 (as n. 37 above).

together selected passages from various places in the text unit (the psalm) into a single location at its beginning. In this, the Paris Psalter is comparable to the illustrations of early biblical manuscripts such as the Ashburnham Pentateuch[41] or the Bible of S. Paolo fuori le mura.[42] Finally, the collective images are organised in part at least as unified compositions in a space that echoes that of landscape, heaven above, earth below. As in the early medieval tradition, earth-strips, one on top of the next, form a series of discontinuous ground lines.

In the Paris Psalter these demarcations are more strongly articulated than those of the earlier manuscripts in the Utrecht Psalter tradition. Each tends to encapsulate a segment of the picture surface, holding the pictorial equivalent of a portion of the psalm text. As a result clear visual instructions about how to 'read' the psalm are provided. Framing each pictorial unit also facilitates meditation on the text evoked by each image. An overlay tracing the visual units reveals the system used, for example, in Psalm 32 (Fig. 21): upper left, '*Rejoice* in the Lord, O just: praise becometh the upright. *Give praise to the Lord on the harp; sing to him with the psaltery, the instrument of ten strings. Sing to him a new canticle, sing well unto him with a loud noise*'; middle left, 'By the *word of the Lord* the heavens were established; and all the power of them by *the spirit of his mouth*' (the artist put books in the hands of the three men as well as Christ above); centre, '*Gathering together the waters of the earth as in a vessel*; laying up the depths in storehouses'; right side in two sections, 'The king is *not saved by a great army: nor shall the giant be saved by his own great strength*'; lower centre, '*Vain is the horse for safety: neither shall he be saved by the abundance of his strength*'; and lower left, 'Behold the eyes of the Lord are on them that fear him: and on *Them that hope in his mercy*. To deliver their souls from death; and *feed them in famine*'.

From Psalm 35 onward the irregularly shaped compartments of the Paris Psalter illustrations were replaced with regular vertical and horizontal subdivisions, sometimes given architectural features, like the conventional framing devices of contemporary manuscripts. The result is one or more horizontal registers in which the individual verbal images are lined up, so that the miniatures look as if they should be read from top to bottom and from left to right, but the pictorial order continues to echo that of the earlier manuscripts in the Utrecht tradition. In the illustration of Psalm 36, for example,[43] the contrast, reiterated throughout the psalm, between the evildoers who may be exalted for a time but will quickly fall and the just who will inherit the land, is approximated by the division between the left and the right on either side of an image of the Lord and the just man whose mouth

40   Vatican, Bibl. Apostolica MS lat. 3225, Italy, fifth century.
41   Paris, Bibl. nationale MS n. a. lat. 2334, provenance uncertain, seventh century.
42   Rome, S. Paolo fuori le mura, Reims, c. 870.
43 · Paris Psalter, fol. 62v; *Psautier illustré* 1906 (as n. 13 above), pl. 45.

shall meditate wisdom and speak judgement (36.30) – the book, the scroll and the scales. The burden of the psalm is that the just shall be filled in the days of famine, that they shall 'inherit the land', a phrase repeated four times (36.9, 11, 29, 34). Perhaps the separated vignettes of food production activities, which are represented in a continuous space in the earlier Utrecht group manuscripts, respond to the repetition of this refrain.

In many illustrations in the Paris Psalter uninscribed scrolls play a part in restoring to the whole some of the fluidity that characterised the earlier manuscripts of the Utrecht Psalter tradition (Figs. 1, 8, 21). They often cut across the individual pictorial-verbal units, connecting the figure holding the scroll with other figures or pictorial elements, and directing the understanding of the viewer. The scrolls represent speech, and might have been intended to be inscribed, as those in the prefatory narratives at the beginning of the manuscript are; and as William Noel has observed, they translate the vocal practice of chanting or reciting the psalms aloud into imagery that stands for the sounding out of the psalter text.[44]

The word-images of the Paris Psalter form compositions referring to the whole of the psalms they precede, even if the individual pictorial motifs do not refer to every single verse. In contrast, the word-images of psalters illustrated with historiated initials at the beginning of each psalm rarely refer to more than a single verse. The physical relation between the illustration and the text block is however complex. Unlike the Paris Psalter, where the psalm illustrations physically parallel the width of the text but are otherwise not integrated with it, the letter-shapes of the historiated initials serve both as textual components and as frames for pictorial subjects. The initials are literally and figuratively embedded in the text, much as they maintain the high visibility that characterises all painted images in written settings.

The physical integration between historiated initial and text no doubt encouraged the selection of pictorial subjects tied to the opening verses of each psalm. In the Twyere Psalter for example, about 65 historiated initials correspond to the opening verses, which typically voice an appeal to the Lord. Of these, more than 40 show the head of God and one or more praying figures, some King David, others naked penitents, sufferers or souls, and many male supplicants of various ages and status, including children, clerics and a warrior. David is the visualisation of the voice of the author of the psalms, often named in the titulus. The other individuals also embody voiced prayer, acting out the feelings of trust, hope, despair, guilt and complaint expressed in the opening lines of the psalms, but they also imply the living supplicant, that is, the user of the book.

Occasionally details of these images correspond with further verses of the psalm. In the Twyere Psalter Psalm 7, for instance (Fig. 22), begins 'O Lord

---

[44]   *Utrecht Psalter* 1996 (as n. 1 above), pp. 159–60.

my God, in thee have I put my trust: save me from all them that persecute me, and deliver me'. The man on his deathbed, eyes closed, corresponds to this plea. The next verse is 'Lest at any time he seize upon my soul like a lion, while there is no one to redeem me, nor to save'. The verbal metaphor of the lion elicits a direct visual translation in the form of the lion menacing the soul of the dying man.

A few historiated initials that show figures in prayer are considerably more complex in the combination of components. One of the most interesting examples is in the Bohun Psalter, in which about 95 psalm illustrations refer to the opening verse, most with representations of praying figures. Psalm 79 (Fig. 23) shows a man in prayer seated under a tree. On the right are a man with a club and the head of a wild beast. Above, on the center axis is the head of God, features rendered invisible by rays. The prayerful man is the 'voice' of the psalm, whose supplication is repeated throughout, from the beginning: 'Give ear, O thou that rulest Israel', to 'O Lord God of Hosts, how long wilt thou be angry against the prayer of thy servant?' (79.5), etc. The man with the club represents verse 7, 'our enemies' who 'have scoffed at us'. The tree is the vine that 'thou plantedst the roots thereof and it filled the land' cited in verses 10–13 and the beast is the 'singular wild beast' that 'hath devoured it [the vine]' of verse 14. The particular form of radiant, veiled face of God corresponds with the words of verse 8, repeated exactly in the last verse (79.20): 'God of hosts, convert us: and shew thy face and we shall be saved'.

Instead of representing the 'I' or 'We' of the psalm, some initials with subjects related to the opening verses show the 'you' or 'they'. For example, the Cuerden Psalter illustration for Psalm 79 (Fig. 24), 'Give ear, O Thou that rulest Israel: thou that leadest Joseph like a sheep' visualises not the supplicant saying 'Give ear' but the object of the prayer, 'Thou that rulest Israel', who is shown in a Jew's hat leading two boys (that is, Joseph, or the children of Israel) while holding a sheep, the literal image of a verbal metaphor.

The illustration for Psalm 71 in the Cuerden Psalter follows the same pattern.[45] It begins, 'Give to the king thy judgment, O God: and to the king's son thy justice: To judge thy people with justice, and thy poor with judgment'. The corresponding initial shows an enthroned man embraced by another man at his side (the king and his son) and then a pictorial example of the just treatment of the poor, with the distribution of bread from a basket held by a smaller, servant figure.

Finally, in some historiated initials the connection with the opening verse of the psalm is abandoned, and the illustrations correspond to words and phrases from later sections. This kind of response to the text, though unusual, is not completely inexplicable. The images quite often are not totally novel

[45]   Cuerden Psalter, fol. 104.

but rather represent the use of familiar pictorial motifs, which appear to be called up by the words of the psalm. For example, the entire theme of Psalm 103 is praise of the blessings of God. In the Twyere Psalter the upper part of illustration for Psalm 103 (Fig. 25) reflects the opening line, 'Bless the Lord, O my soul: O Lord my God, thou art exceedingly great'. But the communion of the skeletal dying man below is a relatively familiar pictorial theme elicited by decontextualising the words of verses 14 and 15: 'That thou mayest bring bread out of the earth: and that wine may cheer the heart of man'. Similarly, in the Cuerden Psalter, verse 30 of Psalm 21 (Fig. 26), 'All the fat ones of the earth have eaten and adored: all they that go down to the earth shall fall before him' seems to have kindled the artist's visual imagination, eliciting the vivid, and well-known, image of the fall of the high and mighty.[46]

Turning again to psalters with marginal illustrations, how does the marginality of such images affect the choice and presentation of their themes? Clearly the physical relation with the words differs from that of psalters illustrated either with full-width miniatures at the beginning of each psalm, or with historiated initials, since, of course, the images are not in the text. Indeed, many times they must be viewed not in terms of the layout of the text but rather the design of the border, where they may constitute discrete elements of a richly varied system of disparate visual motifs; foliate, animal, grotesque, genre, all presented at once. In fact, although it has recently been realised that an unexpectedly large number of marginal images are word-images, and thus charged with 'meaning', the messages of many of the marginal elements sharing the same area of the manuscript page remain elusive.[47]

Actually, the physical presentation of the text exercises considerable control over the themes of marginal word-images. Most of them are associated with the first or the last lines on a page. The words at the beginning or end of any page fall there by accident, so the artist is in a position to 'see' the visual potential of a different portion of the text with each manuscript that he illuminates. Further, the fact that a particular page may begin with the tail of a verse or break off before the end of a verse is conducive to the decontextualisation of marginal word-images.

Of the English psalters with profuse marginal word-illustrations, only the Luttrell Psalter has images in the side margins. Some of these belong to the

[46]   E.g., Luttrell Psalter, fol. 53, Psalm 27.1, 'them that go down [descendentibus] into the pit'; Luttrell Psalter 1932 (as n. 7 above), pl. 8. Cf. the Tree of Vices in the Vergier de soulas, a French collection of pictorial diagrams of c. 1290 (Paris, Bibl. nationale MS fr. 9220, fol. 6), in which Pride, the root vice, is pictured as a man falling from a horse at the bottom of the tree; see L. F. Sandler, The Psalter of Robert de Lisle in the British Library, London 1983, pp. 137–8.

[47]   See L. F. Sandler, 'The Study of Marginal Imagery: Past, Present, and Future', Studies in Iconography 18, 1997, pp. 1–49.

standard word-image repertory; a fool, the pelican and the sparrow, the murdered widow and children, and musicians, for example. Even if the source-word is in the middle of a line in the middle of the page, the mental association of word and image was strong enough to elicit the picture. In other cases, however, the vertical spaces of the side margins proved to be areas susceptible to the invention of new images sparked by words, primarily verbs, of direction, going up, going down. 'Them that go down into the pit' (Descentibus in lacum) of Psalm 27 elicits a standard image of a man falling from a horse,[48] but elsewhere similar terms are linked with new, imaginative fantasies such as the one adjacent to Psalm 29:4 (Fig. 27) where an elongated female hybrid pours a stream of white liquid, perhaps a syllabic pun on 'lac' (milk), down the length of the margin in response to 'Thou hast brought forth, O Lord, my soul from hell: thou hast saved me from them that *go down* into the *pit*'.[49] Hybrids that correspond to words and phrases in the text are ubiquitous in marginal imagery, confirming Michael Camille's conclusion that 'at the edge he [the artist] was free to read the words for himself and make what he wanted of them'.[50]

Similar pictorial motifs recur in the illustrations of psalters widely distant in date and different in format, raising a question of the transmission of word-images. Traditionally for example, investigation of the four psalters that constitute the Utrecht Psalter group has focused on their pictorial interrelationships, using a philological approach to construct a stemma of manuscripts.[51] Although the method was borrowed from philology, the result was to treat pictorial imagery as divorced from the text. In other words, once the pictorial corpus was first created, whether in the fifth or the ninth century, the illustrations of succeeding manuscripts were thought to copy or interpret pictorial models, and seldom, if ever, to refer back to the text of the psalms. However, this schema has been challenged by William Noel,[52] and, in fact, study of word illustration in the later books descended from the Utrecht Psalter offers abundant evidence that the responsiveness of artists to the text resulted in images that differ from manuscript to manuscript.

Yet there are also striking instances where visual agreement extends beyond the manuscripts of the Utrecht Psalter group to encompass later psalters that differ completely in format. For example, the 'hart' that 'panteth after water' illustrates Psalm 41 in the Paris Psalter,[53] the Cuerden Psalter (Fig.

[48] See note 46.
[49] Psalm 29.4: 'Domine eduxisti ad inferno animam meam; salvasti me a *descendentibus in lacum*'.
[50] Camille 1992 (as n. 35 above), p. 42.
[51] For a recent summary and evaluation of opinions, and extensive bibliography, see *Utrecht Psalter* 1996 (as n. 1 above).
[52] *Utrecht Psalter* 1996 (as n. 1 above), pp. 125–9.
[53] Paris Psalter, fol. 73v; see *Psautier illustré* 1906 (as n. 13 above), pl. 50, painted by

28), the Twyere Psalter,[54] the Bohun Psalter,[55] and also all the extant thirteenth-century French psalters with literal illustrations, even the psalms in the Bible moralisée.[56] Such universal agreement was undoubtedly conditioned by the simile embedded in the text; 'As the hart panteth after the fountains of water; so my soul panteth after thee, O God', the basis of the standard exegesis in terms of human longing for Christ, the Fountain of Life.

But some recurrent illustrations do not carry the symbolic weight of the hart and the water. Psalm 40, for example, is illustrated in the French manuscripts and in the Paris Psalter (Fig. 29),[57] the Twyere Psalter (Fig. 30), as well as the Bohun Psalter[58] with scenes of distribution of bread or clothing, examples drawn from the opening line, 'Blessed is he that understandeth concerning the needy and the poor'.[59] What is the explanation of the parallels among these images? Was the transmission visual, that is, dependent on pictorial models; or textual, that is, dependent on familiarity with verbal interpretations, whether full-scale commentaries or simple instruction lists; or cultural-dependent on remembered (that is, memorial) images, a process by which certain words or phrases habitually elicited the same mental pictures over centuries?

Although answers to this question would be conjectural in relation to the surviving examples of English psalters with literal illustrations, there is

---

the mid-fourteenth century Catalan artist who completed the illustrations, here working over drawings of the original artist; on the later hand see M. Meiss, 'Italian Style in Catalonia and a Fourteenth-Century Catalan Workshop', *Journal of the Walters Art Gallery* 4, 1941, pp. 45–87.

[54] Twyere Psalter, fol. 75.

[55] Bohun Psalter, fol. 40.

[56] Bible moralisée, Paris, Bibl. nationale MS lat. 11560, fol. 12, Paris, *c.* 1220–30; see A. Laborde, *Étude sur la Bible moralisée*, Paris 1911–27, pl. 236. On French psalters with literal illustrations for every psalm see E. Peterson, 'Iconography of the Historiated Psalm Initials in the Thirteenth-Century French Fully-Illustrated Psalter Group', Ph.D. diss., University of Pittsburgh 1991; idem, 'Accidents in Transmission among Fully-Illustrated Thirteenth-Century French Psalters', *Zeitschrift für Kunstgeschichte* 50, 1987, pp. 375–84, and 'The Textual Basis for Visual Errors in French Gothic Psalter Illustration', in *The Early Medieval Bible, Its Production, Decoration and Use*, R. Gameson (ed.), Cambridge 1994, pp. 177–204.

[57] In the Paris Psalter Psalm 40 was painted by the mid-fourteenth century Catalan artist over drawings by the original artist; see note 53 above.

[58] Bohun Psalter, fol. 39v.; see M. R. James and E. G. Millar, *The Bohun Manuscripts*, Oxford 1936, pl. 43c.

[59] See also the historiated initial for Psalm 40 in the Luttrell Psalter (fol. 79v), with two ill-clothed beggars rejected by a richly dressed man; for a reproduction see L. F. Sandler, 'Pictorial and Verbal Play in the Margins: The case of British Library, Stowe MS 49', in *Illuminating the Book, Makers and Interpreters, Essays in Honour of Janet Backhouse*, M. P. Brown and S. McKendrick (eds), London 1998, fig. 19.

evidence from across the Channel that one means by which identical word images were produced in French psalters was verbal.[60] Lists of subjects and marginal 'instructions' in either Latin or French, all similar, support the idea of an established pictorial tradition for literal psalter illustration that was maintained not through pictorial models or mental images but through verbal sources.[61] For example, the Latin instructions for the illustration of Psalm 40 are 'David dat pauperi panem',[62] corresponding closely with the actors and the action in the French psalters.[63]

Such verbal sources do not survive in England, and indeed the thirteenth- and fourteenth-century English psalters with literal illustrations do not form an iconographically cohesive group, since they have many more unique images than the French books. Nevertheless, some words, and even some phrases were nearly universally favoured for illustration, and the resulting images turn out to be identical in theme. What has been somewhat overlooked as a possible explanation is the factor of culturally based concepts retained in the mind in the form of images. Artists did not have to read anything to represent the needy and the poor of Psalm 40 with a scene of distribution of bread, alms or clothing. Such pictures would be recalled instantaneously from the shared fund of mental images that constituted the concept of Christian Charity throughout the Middle Ages.[64]

[60] See Peterson 1987, 1991 and 1994 (as n. 56 above).

[61] The chief French manuscripts with historiated initials for all the psalms and *tituli*, 'instructions', or separate lists of subjects are: Manchester, John Rylands Lib. MS 22, c.1225–30; St. Petersburg, Saltykov-Scedrin State Public Lib. MS Q.v.I.67, c.1225–30; Philadelphia, Free Lib., Lewis Coll. MS 185, c.1235; Cambridge, University Lib. MS Ee.iv.24, c.1280; Paris, Bibl. nationale MS lat. 10435, c.1295 (the dates are those suggested by Peterson 1995 [as n. 56 above], pp. 178–9). See also S. Berger, 'Les manuels pour l'illustration du psautier au xiiie siècle', *Mémoires de la Société nationale des antiquaires de France* 6th ser., 7, 1898, pp. 95–134.

[62] Manchester, John Rylands Lib. MS 22. fol. 51v; for the full list see M. R. James, *A Descriptive Catalogue of the Latin Manuscripts in the John Rylands Library at Manchester*, Manchester 1921, vol. 1, pp. 68–70. Cf. Cambridge, University Lib. MS Ee.iv.24, fol. 13v, with an illustration of David distributing bread and on fol. 4, in a separate list of *tituli*, 'David done le pain au poure'; see M. R. James, 'On a Ms. Psalter in the University Library', *Proceedings of the Cambridge Antiquarian Society, 1892–1893* 8, 1894, pp. 146–67. I am grateful to Professor Elizabeth Peterson for providing additional information about these manuscripts.

[63] In the English manuscripts considered here the actors are more varied: the Paris Psalter shows the man of understanding blessed by the hand of God seated next to a container from which loaves of bread are distributed by another man to two poor men (Fig. 29); the Cuerden Psalter shows two men distributing bread to two poor men (Fig. 30); the Bohun Psalter shows a secular rider giving bread to a bare-chested man (James and Millar 1936 [as n. 58 above], pl. 43c).

[64] For recent studies see M. Mollat, *The Poor in the Middle Age: An Essay in Social*

As a mode of psalter illustration, *imagines verborum* evoke a final question: what was the impact of such literal imagery on looking, reading and remembering, in short, on the use of the book to its possessor? Psalters with literal illustrations are by definition luxury books; the material expense of producing at least 150 images was considerable, especially in the case of these Gothic manuscripts, since all the illustrations were on gold backgrounds. The manuscripts were meant for wealthy owners, whether clerical or secular. How were such manuscripts used? This, of course, is a question that relates to all luxury manuscripts. And as in other cases, the answers here are varied: for instance, the Paris Psalter has an elaborate textual apparatus, echoing that of the Eadwine Psalter, but unlike the earlier twelfth-century book it may not have been used for monastic study, and its splendid illustrations suggest that it might have been destined for a royal owner,[65] perhaps more to be read and appreciated in some court circle than in private devotions. The Twyere Psalter contains antiphons in the original hand, and the antiphons were added in the fourteenth century in the margins of the Bohun Psalter, suggesting possible use in conjunction with religious services, during which antiphons were sung before and after groups of psalms.[66] The Luttrell Psalter, nearly as large in dimensions as the Paris Psalter, with an ungraded calendar, and with innumerable pictorial and heraldic references to the Luttrell family, has the earmarks of a 'family treasure', to be pored over like a photograph album rather than to serve as a devotional aid on a prie-dieu in a private chapel, or on the lectern of a choir stall.

In view of this variety of projected uses we may ask again how word illustrations functioned. To the extent that the images glossed the text pictorially they mimicked the role of verbal glosses, transforming the text into an object of study, and deepening the experience of reading and understanding the words. The visualisation of nouns and verbs used metaphorically in the psalms, resulting in striking and memorable images, might ultimately lead to remembering the text, but in the first instance they would encourage an individual to read through the text to find the verbal analogue in its scriptural setting. Even more so would the owner of a psalter with completely decontextualised word images in the margins be challenged to engage in the activity of seeking out the relevant words in the text and discovering the riches of meaning concealed therein.

Probably those who owned these manuscripts had heard the psalms chanted, perhaps they themselves sounded the words aloud as they looked at these books, but *imagines verborum* gave them the opportunity to 'read' both

History, New Haven and London 1986; and G. B. Guest, 'A Discourse on the Poor: The Hours of Jeanne d'Evereux', *Viator* 26, 1995, pp. 145–80.
[65] *Utrecht Psalter* 1996 (as n. 1 above), p. 240.
[66] See A. Hughes, *Medieval Manuscripts for Mass and Office. A Guide to their Organization and Terminology*, Toronto 1982, p. 232.

text and images reciprocally, using the faculty of sight. If the words gave rise to the images, the images disclosed the depths of meaning in the text. In sum, for the thirteenth and fourteenth centuries images of words enhanced the experience of reading the psalms and made it rewarding spiritually.

Meehan 1. Book of Kells, *Magnificat*. Dublin, Trinity Coll. MS A.I.6, fol. 191v (photo: Trinity Coll.).

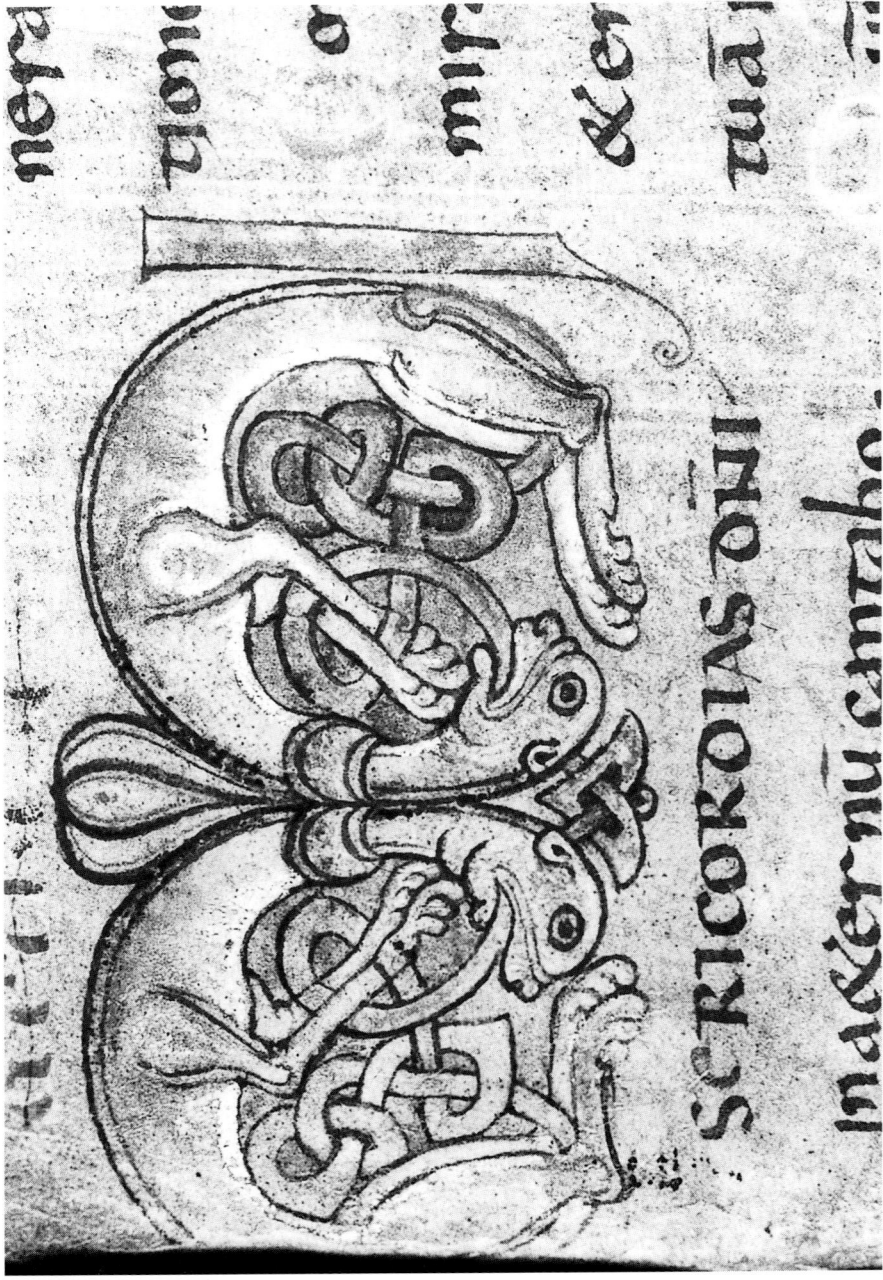

Meehan 2. Corbie Psalter, *Misericordias*. Amiens, Bibl. municipale MS 18, fol. 80r (photo: Bibl. municipale).

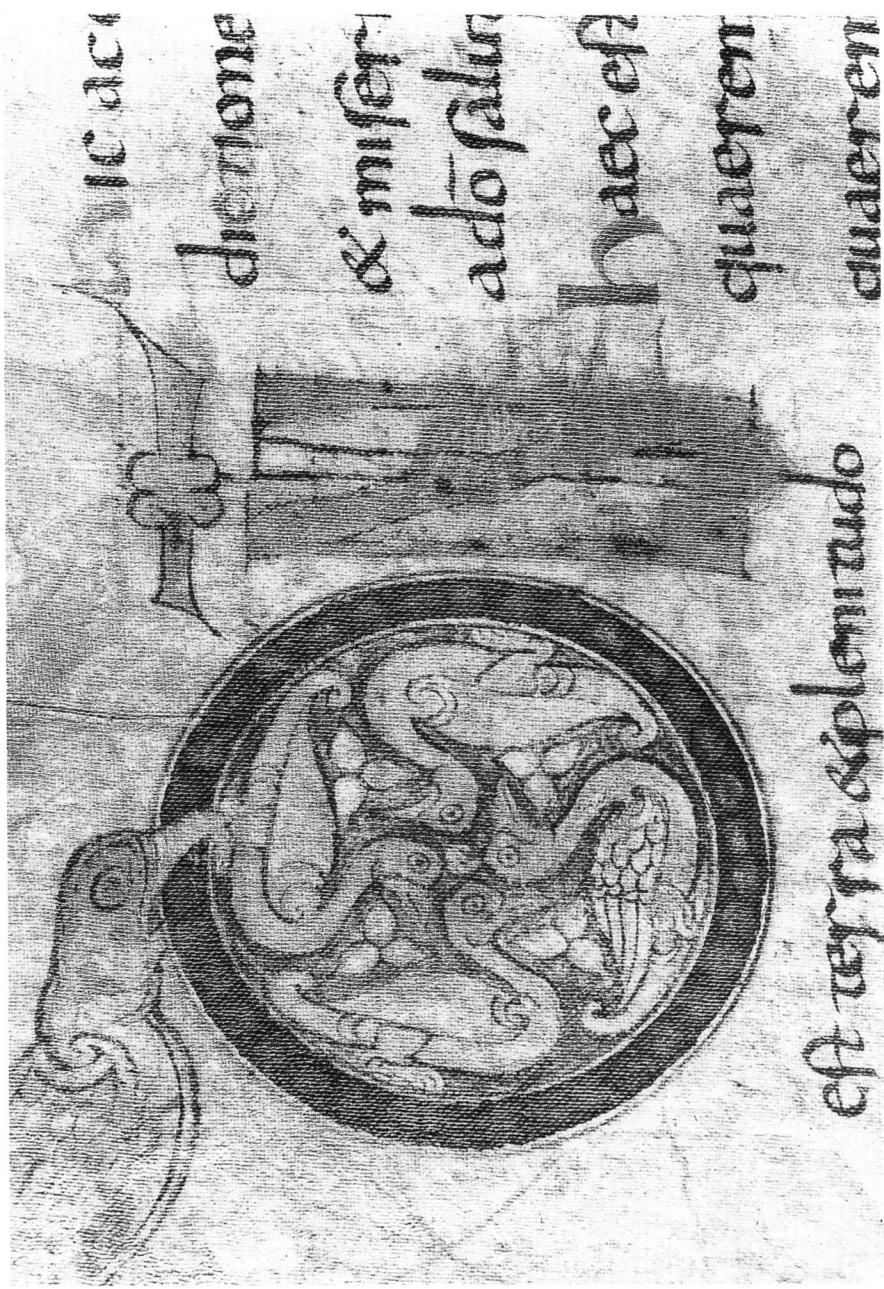

Meehan 3. Corbie Psalter. Amiens, Bibl. municipale MS 18, fol. 20v (photo: Bibl. municipale).

Meehan 4. Book of Kells. Dublin, Trinity Coll. MS A.I.6, fol. 152v
(photo: Trinity Coll.).

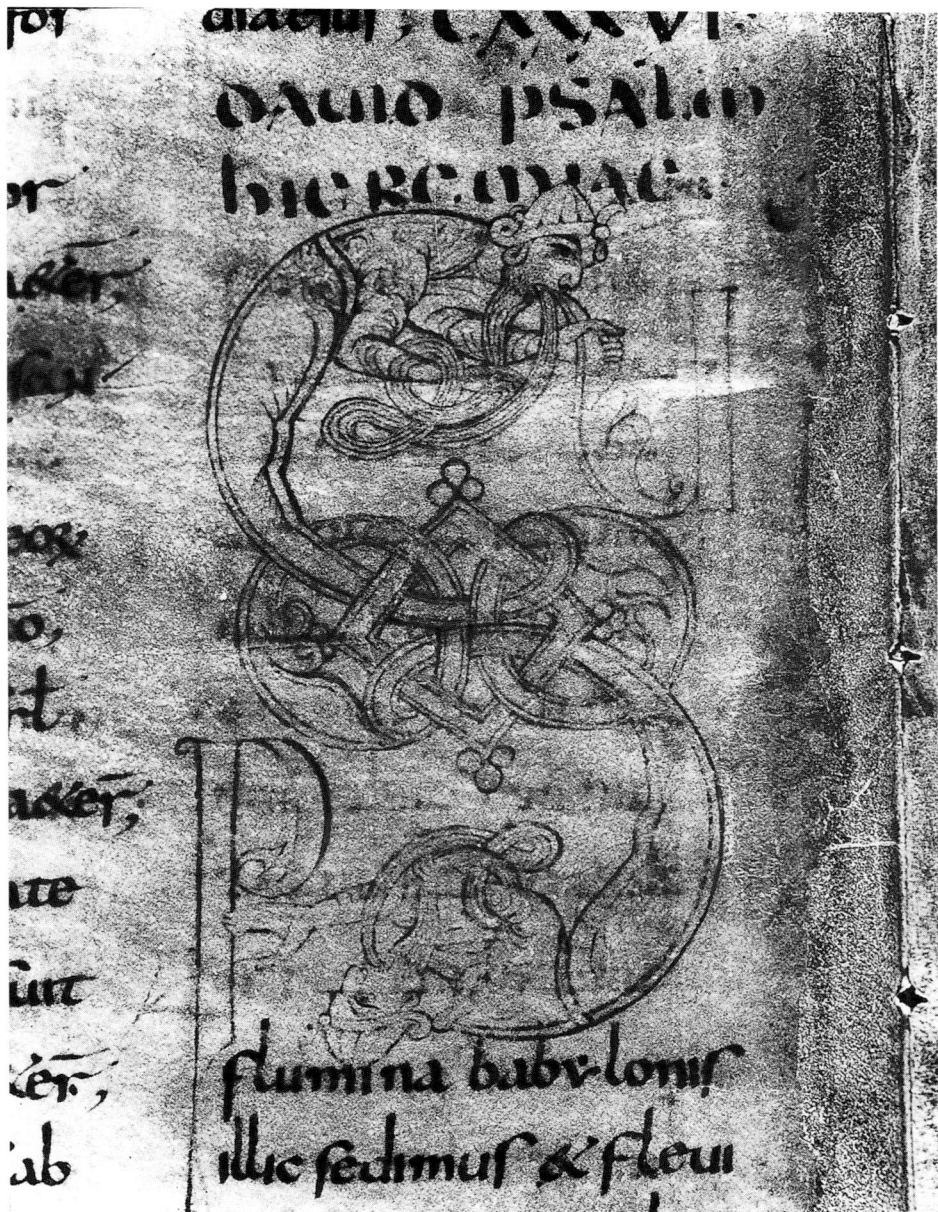

Meehan 5. Corbie Psalter. Amiens, Bibl. municipale MS 18, fol. 113v
(photo: Bibl. municipale).

Meehan 6 (opposite, top). Book of Kells. Dublin, Trinity Coll. MS A.I.6, fol. 53v (photo: Trinity Coll.).

Meehan 7 (opposite, bottom). Corbie Psalter. Amiens, Bibl. municipale MS 18, fol. 92r (photo: Bibl. municipale).

Meehan 8 (above). Book of Kells. Dublin, Trinity Coll. MS A.I.6, fol. 252v (photo: Trinity Coll.).

Meehan 9. Book of Kells. Dublin, Trinity Coll. MS A.I.6, fol. 188r
(photo: Trinity Coll.).

Meehan 10 (opposite). Detail from the same page.

Meehan 11. Corbie Psalter, Amiens, Bibl. municipale MS 18, fol. 110r (photo: Bibl. municipale).

Meehan 12. Book of Kells. Dublin, Trinity Coll. MS A.I.6, fol. 124r
(photo: Trinity Coll.).

Meehan 13 (opposite). Detail from the same page.

Meehan 14. Corbie Psalter. Amiens, Bibl. municipale MS 18, fol. 73r
(photo: Bibl. municipale).

Meehan 15. Corbie Psalter. Amiens, Bibl. municipale MS 18, fol. 123v
(photo: Bibl. municipale).

Pulliam 1. Corbie Psalter, Psalm 1. Amiens, Bibl. municipale MS 18, fol. 1v
(photo: Bibl. municipale)

Pulliam 2 (left). Corbie Psalter, Psalm 31. Amiens, Bibl. municipale MS 18, fol. 26v (photo: Bibl. municipale)

Pulliam 3 (below, left). Corbie Psalter, Psalm 57. Amiens, Bibl. municipale MS 18, fol. 50v (photo: Bibl. municipale)

Pulliam 4 (below, right). Book of Kells. Dublin, Trinity Coll. MS A.I.6, fol. 122r (photo: Trinity Coll.)

Pulliam 5. Corbie Psalter, Psalm 9. Amiens, Bibl. municipale MS 18, fol. 7v (photo: Bibl. municipale)

Pulliam 6. Corbie Psalter, Psalm 72. Amiens, Bibl. municipale MS 18, fol. 101r (photo: Bibl. municipale)

Pulliam 7. Corbie
Psalter, Psalm 61.
Amiens, Bibl.
municipale MS 18,
fol. 53r (photo:
Bibl. municipale)

Pulliam 8. Corbie
Psalter, Psalm 108.
Amiens, Bibl.
municipale MS 18,
fol. 92v (photo:
Bibl. municipale)

Noel 1. Psalm 39. Baltimore, Walters Art Gallery MS W.88, fol. 150v
(photo: Walters Art Gall.)

Noel 2. Annunciation. Baltimore, Walters Art Gallery MS W.82, fol. 171r
(photo: Walters Art Gall.)

Noel 3. Utrecht Psalter, Canticle of Habbakuk. Utrecht, Rijksuniversiteit Bibl. MS 32, fol 85v (detail) (photo: Rijksuniversiteit Bibl.)

Noel 4. Utrecht Psalter, Psalm 108. Utrecht, Rijksuniversiteit Bibl. MS 32, fol. 64r (detail) (photo: Rijksuniversiteit Bibl.)

DELAPIDEPRETIOSO
UITAMPETIITATEETTRI
BUISTIEI LONGITUDI
NEMDIERUMINSAE
CULUMETINSAECULI

MOUEBITUR
INUIRTUTERMANUS
TUAOMNIBUSINIMICIS
TUIS DEXTERATUAIN
UENIATOMNESQUITE
ODERUNT

INRELIQUIISTUISPRAE
PARABISUULTUMEORU
EXALTAREDNEINUIR
TUTITUACANTABI
MUSETPSALLIMUSUIR
TUTESTUAS

XXIINFINEMPRO ADSUMPTIONE ORATIONAPSALOO

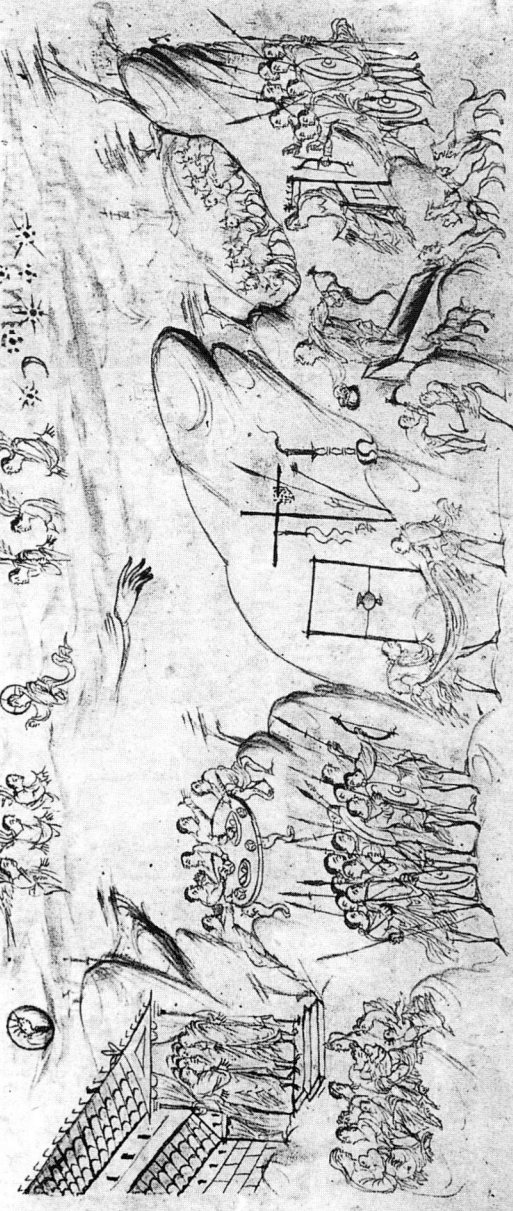

Noel 5. Utrecht Psalter, Psalm 21. Utrecht, Rijksuniversiteit Bibl. MS 32, fol. 12r (detail) (photo: Rijksuniversiteit Bibl.)

Noel 6. London, British Lib. MS Cotton Titus D.xxvii, fol. 75v. (photo: British Lib.)

SOL · IVNA · SCĀ MARIA · SCĪ IOHANNES ·

Kidd 1. London, British Lib. MS Arundel 60, fol. 12v
(photo: Courtauld Institute, Conway Library)

Kidd 2. London, British Lib. MS Arundel 60, fol. 52v
(photo: Courtauld Institute, Conway Library)

B	VI	D	V	I	D	V	P	D	V	P	D	V
	VII	V	H	D	V	O	D	V	O	D	V	O
	I	H	B	I	H	C	I	H	C	I	H	H
	II	A	S	G	A	S	M	B	S	M	B	S
B	IIII	Q	E	Ẏ	Q	L	W	Q	M	E	Q	L
	V	E	X	Q	K	L	Q	K	L	Q	K	E
	VI	V	P	I	X	P	I	K	P	I	K	V
	VII	O	D	C	O	H	C	O	H	C	O	H
B	II	B	S	M	G	A	M	G	A	M	G	A
	III	R	M	F	I	M	F	I	M	F	I	R
	IIII	L	E	Ẏ	L	E	Ẏ	L	F	Ẏ	Q	E
	V	L	Q	K	E	X	K	E	X	K	E	X
B	VII	O	H	C	V	H	D	V	O	D	V	O
	I	h⊧	B	I	H	B	I	H	C	I	H	C
	II	A	M	G	A	S	G	A	S	R	B	S
	III	M	F	T	R	E	I	R	M	I	B	M
B	V	E	X	Q	E	X	Q	K	L	Q	K	L
	VI	V	P	D	V	P	D	V	P	I	K	P
	VII	O	D	V	O	D	V	O	H	C	O	H
	I	C	I	H	C	I	H	h	I	H	K	B
B	III	R	M	F	R	M	E	I	M	F	I	M
	IIII	L	W	Q	L	E	Q	L	F	Ẏ	L	E
	V	L	Q	K	L	Q	I	E	X	K	E	X
	VI	P	L	K	P	I	K	V	I	D	V	I
B	I	H	B	H	H	B	I	H	B	I	H	C
	II	A	M	G	A	O	G	I	S	G	A	S
	III	M	F	I	M	F	I	R	F	I	R	M
	IIII	E	Ẏ	L	E	Ẏ	Q	F	Ẏ	Q	E	Ẏ

Kidd 3. London, British Lib. MS Arundel 60, fol. 11v
(photo: Courtauld Institute, Conway Library)

Backhouse 1. Burdett Psalter-Hours. Private Collection, fol. 7r

Backhouse 2. Burdett Psalter-Hours. Private Collection, fol. 8v

Backhouse 3. Burdett Psalter-Hours. Private Collection, fol. 9r

Backhouse 4. Burdett Psalter-Hours. Private Collection, fol. 10v

Backhouse 5. Burdett Psalter-Hours. Private Collection, fol. 11r

Backhouse 6. Burdett Psalter-Hours. Private Collection, fol. 12r.

tatis uir qui non abijt i
consilio impior z in uia pec
catorum ñ stetit: z in cathe
dra pestilentie non sedit.
Sed in lege dñi uoluntas
eius: et in lege eius medita
bitur die ac nocte. Et erit
tanquam lignum quod plan
tatum est secus decursus a
quarum qd fructu suu dabit
in tempore suo. Et foliu
eius non defluet: et oñia quecunq; faciet psperabuntr.
Non sic impij non sic: s; tanq pulius quam picit ue
tus a facie terre. Ideo non resurgunt impij in iudicio
neq; peccatores in consilio iustorum. Quonia nouit dñs
uiam iustorum: et iter impiorum peribit. Psalmus ij.
Quare fremuerunt gentes: et populi meditati sunt i
uania. Astiterunt reges terre et principes conuenerut
inunum aduersus dñm: et aduersus xpm eius. Dis
rumpamus uincula eorum: et piciamus a nobis iugu
ipsorum. Qui habitat in celis inridebit eos: et dñs sub
sannabit eos. Tunc loquetur ad eos in ira sua: et i
furore suo conturbabit eos. Ego autem constitutus
sum rex ab eo sup syon montem scm eius pdicans preptu eius.
Dñs dixit ad me fili ms es tu: ego hodie genui te. Po
stula a me et dabo tibi gentes hereditatem tua: z pos
sessionem tua terminos terre. Reges eos in uirga ferrea:
et tanq uas figuli confringes eos. Et nunc reges i
telligite: erudimini qui iudicatis terram. Seruite do
mino in timore: et exultate ei cum tremore. Apprehen

Backhouse 8. Burdett Psalter-Hours, Psalm 52. Private Collection, fol. 34r

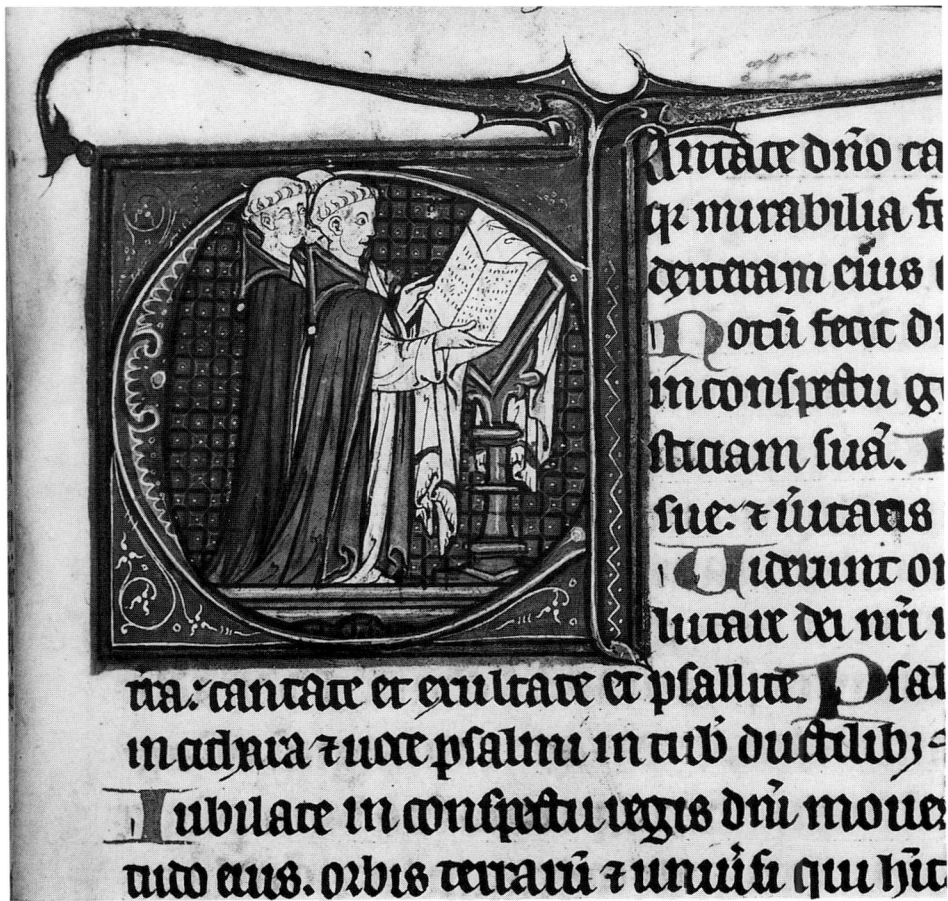

antate dño ca
qi mirabilia fi
dexteram eius (
Notū fecit dī
in conspectu g
stītiam suā. I
sue: ꝉ iustītīas
Uiderunt ō
lutare dei nr̄i i

tia. cantate et exultate et psallite. Psal
in cithara ꝉ uoce psalmi in tub ductilib;
Iubilate in conspectu regis dñi moue
tudo eius. oxbis terrarū ꝉ unuisi qui hīc

Backhouse 9. Burdett Psalter-Hours, Psalm 97. Private Collection, fol. 52r

Backhouse 10. Burdett Psalter-Hours, Psalm 109. Private Collection, fol. 58r

Backhouse 11. Burdett Psalter-Hours. Private Collection, fol. 77r

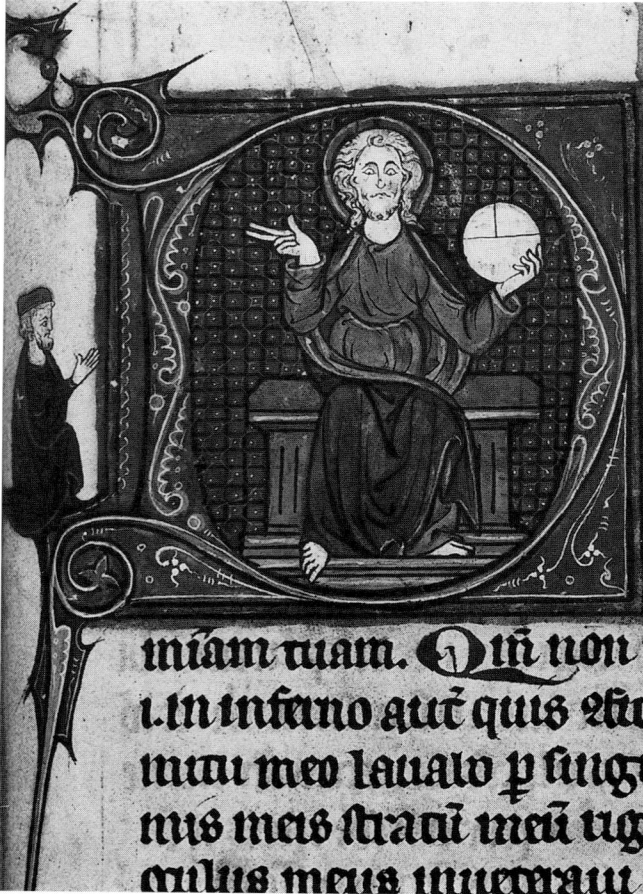

Backhouse 12. Burdett Psalter-Hours. Private Collection, fol. 90r

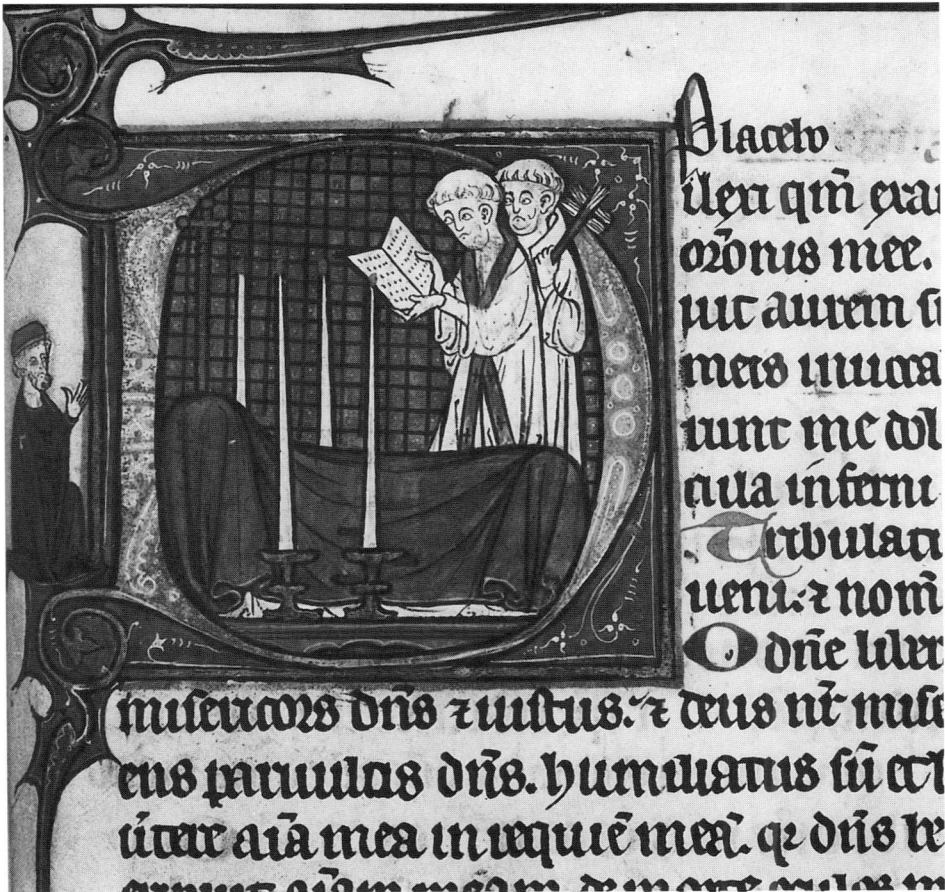

Backhouse 13. Burdett Psalter-Hours. Private Collection, fol. 96r

Sandler 1. Paris Psalter, Psalm 8. Paris, Bibl. nationale MS lat. 8846, fol. 14v (from Omont 1906, pl. 17)

Sandler 2. Paris Psalter, Psalm 22. Paris, Bibl. nationale MS lat. 8846, fol. 39v (from Omont 1906, pl. 31)

Sandler 3 (right). Cuerden Psalter, Psalm 44. New York, Pierpont Morgan Lib. MS M.756, fol. 68v (photo: Pierpont Morgan Lib.)

Sandler 4 (below). Twyere Psalter, Psalm 8. New York, New York Public Lib. MS Spencer 2, fol. 21v (photo: New York Public Lib.)

Sandler 5 (below, bottom). Twyere Psalter, Psalm 22. New York, New York Public Lib. MS Spencer 2, fol. 43v (photo: New York Public Lib.)

Sandler 6. Bohun Psalter, Psalm 10. Vienna Österreichische Nationalbibl. cod. 1826*, fol. 13
(photo: Bildarchiv, ÖNB Wein)

Sandler 7. Twyere Psalter, Psalm 142. New York, New York Public Lib. MS Spencer 2, fol. 222 (photo: New York Public Lib.)

Sandler 9. Cuerden Psalter, Psalm 78. New York, Pierpont Morgan Lib. MS M.756, fol. 120 (photo: Pierpont Morgan Lib.)

Sandler 8. Paris Psalter, Psalm 25 (detail).
Paris, Bibl. nationale MS lat. 8846, fol. 43v (from Omont 1906, pl. 34)

Sandler 10. Bohun Psalter, Psalm 125 (above). Vienna, Österreichische Nationalbibl. cod. 1826*, fol. 114 (photo: Bildarchiv ÖNB Wien)

Effabuntur et loquentur iniquitatem:
loquentur omnes qui operantur in
iusticiam

Populum tuum domine humilia
uerunt: 7 hereditatem tuam ueraucrūt.
Uiduam 7 aduenam interfecerunt et
pupillos occiderunt.

Et dixerunt non uidebit dominus:
nec intelliget deus iacob.

Intelligite insipientes in populo: et
stulti aliquando sapite.

Qui plantauit aurem non audiet:
aut qui finxit oculum non considerat.

Qui corripit gentes non arguet: qui

Sandler 11. Luttrell Psalter, Psalm 93. London, British Lib. MS Add. 42130, fol. 169
(photo: British Lib.)

dat eum: † in laqueum cadat in ipsū.
Anima autem mea exultabit in do
mino: † delectabitur super salutari
suo.

Omnia ossa mea dicent: domine
quis similis sit tibi.

Eripiens inopem de manu forcio
rum eius: egenum † pauperem a
diripientibus eum.

Surgentes testes iniqui: que igno
rabant interrogabant me.

Retribuebant michi mala pro bo
nis: sterilitatem anime mee.

Ego autem cum michi molesti es

Sandler 12. Luttrell Psalter, Psalm 34.13. London, British Lib. MS Add. 42130, fol. 66 (detail)
(photo: British Lib.)

Sandler 13. Cuerden Psalter, Psalm 16. New York, Pierpont Morgan Lib. MS M.756, fol. 25v (photo: Pierpont Morgan Lib.)

Sandler 14. Cuerden Psalter, Psalm 11.
New York, Pierpont Morgan Lib.
MS M.756, fol. 21v
(photo: Pierpont Morgan Lib.)

Sandler 15. Bohun Psalter, Psalm 36. Vienna, Österreichische Nationalbibl. cod. 1826*, fol. 35
(photo: Bildarchiv ÖNB Wein)

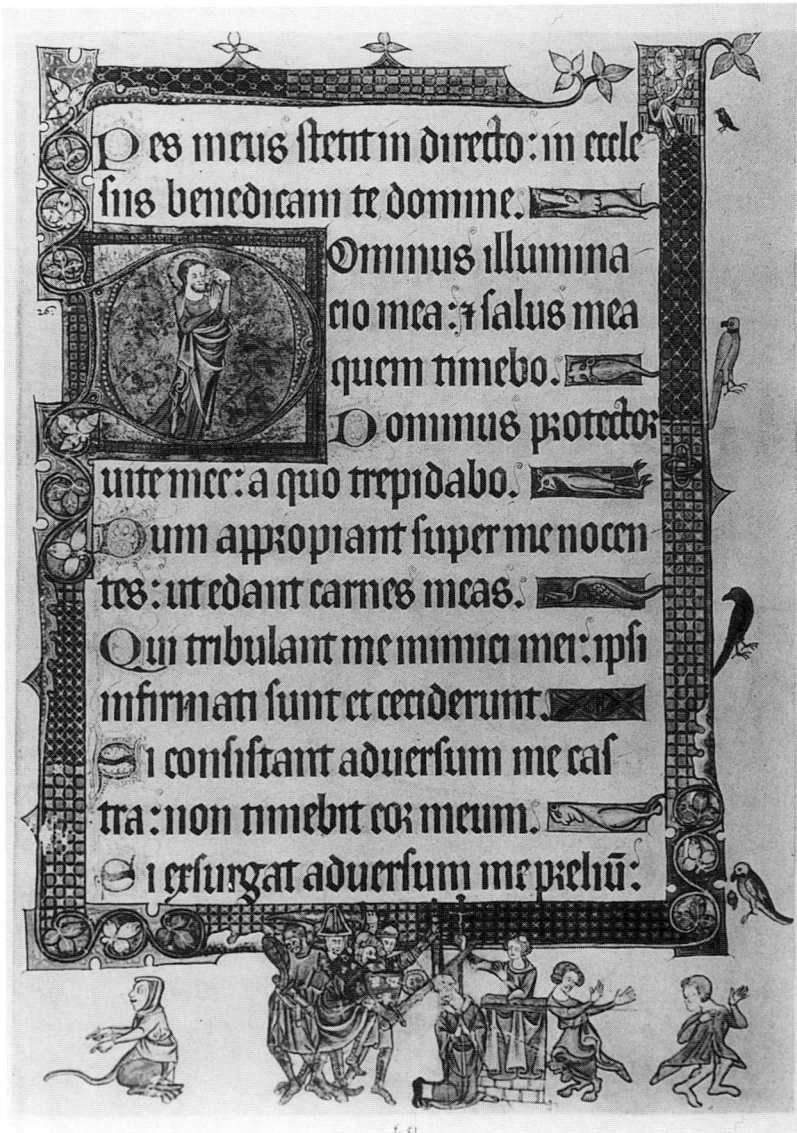

Pes meus stetit in directo: in ecclesiis benedicam te domine.

Dominus illumina cio mea: ⁊ salus mea quem timebo.

Dominus protector uite mee: a quo trepidabo.

Dum appropiant super me nocentes: ut edant carnes meas.

Qui tribulant me inimici mei: ipsi infirmati sunt et ceciderunt.

Si consistant aduersum me castra: non timebit cor meum.

Si exsurgat aduersum me prelium:

Sandler 16. Luttrell Psalter, Psalm 26. London, British Lib. MS Add. 42130, fol. 51
(from Millar 1932, pl. 7)

bulabunt: + in nomine tuo exultabunt
tota die. + in iusticia tua exaltabuntur.
Quoniam gloria uirtutis eorum tu
es: + in beneplacito tuo exaltabitur
cornu nostrum.

Quia domini est assumpcio nostra:
+ sancti israel regis nostri.

Tunc locutus es in uisione sanctis tu
is + dixisti: posui adiutorium in poten
te. + exaltaui electum de plebe mea.

Inueni dauid seruum meum: oleo
sancto meo unxi eum.

Manus enim mea auxiliabitur ei: et
brachium meum confirmabit eum.

Sandler 17. Luttrell Psalter, Psalm 88. London, British Lib. MS Add. 42130, fol. 160v
(from Millar 1932, pl. 73)

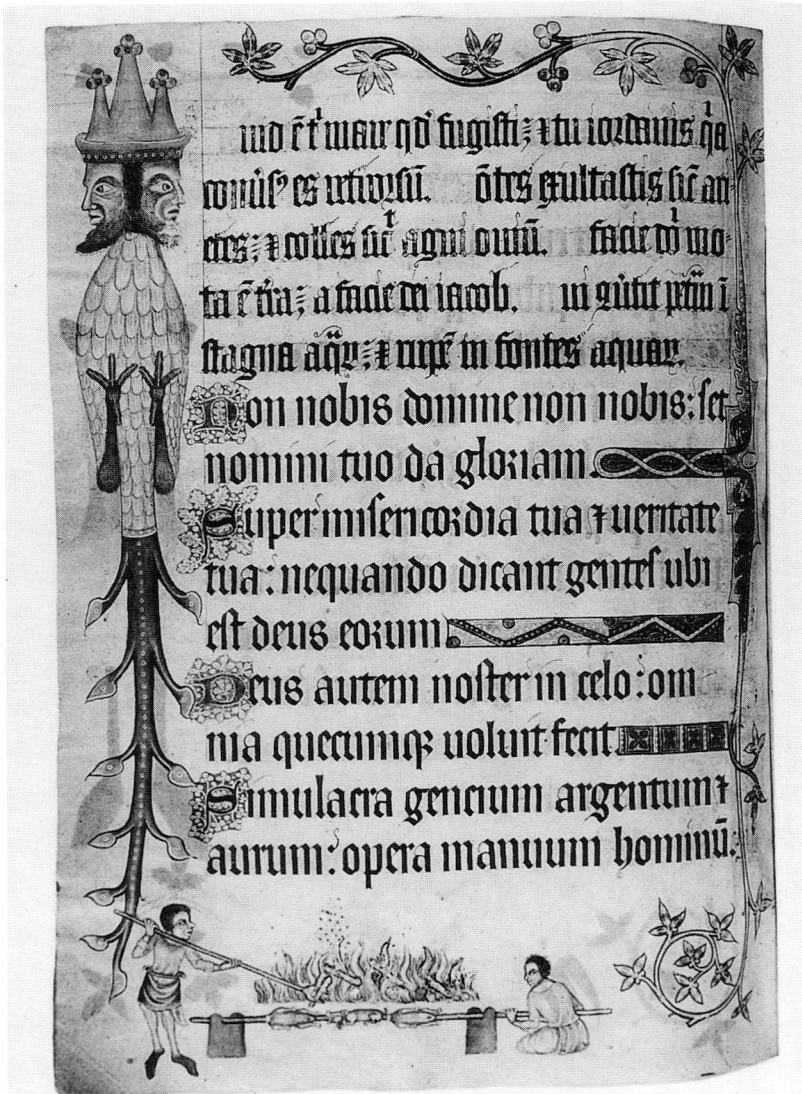

uo é t mar qd fugifti; ⁊ tu iozdanis ḣa
conuſ° es uriozſu. õtrs gultaſtis ſ̄i an
etes; ⁊ coltes ſ̄i agni ouū. facite dō mo
ta é tua; a facie dei iacob. in giúit prin i
ſtagna aq̈r; ⁊ ruẏr in fontes aquar.

Non nobis dō̄e non nobis: ſet
nom̄u tuo da gloriam.

Super miſericordia tua ⁊ ueritate
tua: nequando dicant gentes ubi
eſt deus eorum.

Deus autem noſter in celo: om
ma quecum⸗ uoluit fecit.

Simulacra gencium argentum ⁊
aurum: opera manuum hominū.

Sandler 18. Luttrell Psalter, Psalm 113. London, British Lib. MS Add. 42130, fol. 206v
(photo: British Lib.)

Sandler 19. Twyere Psalter, Psalm 83. New York, New York Public Lib. MS Spencer 2, fol. 141 (photo: New York Public Lib.)

Sandler 20. Luttrell Psalter, Psalm 83. London, British Lib. MS Add. 42130, fol. 83 (detail) (from Millar 1932, pl. 57)

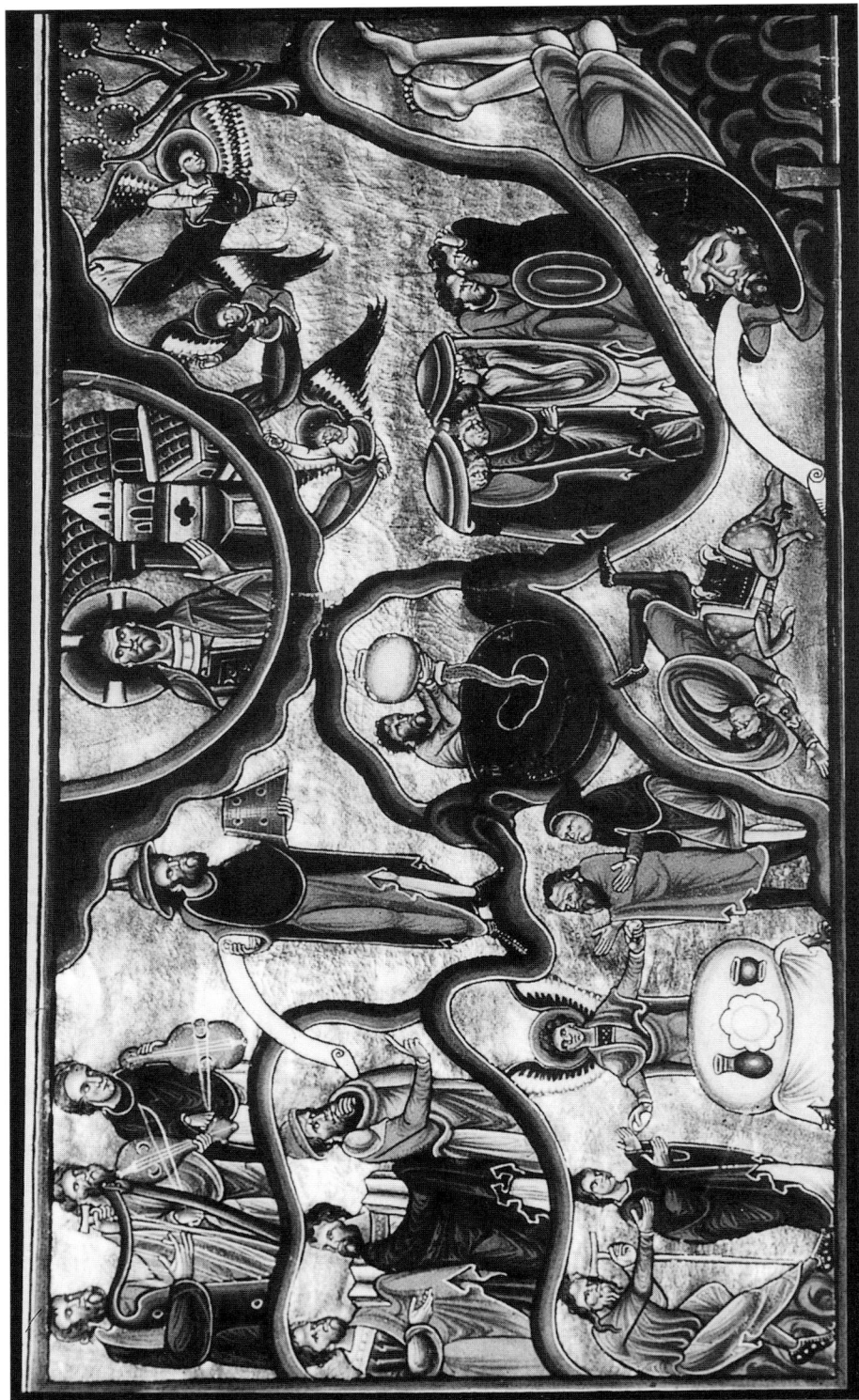

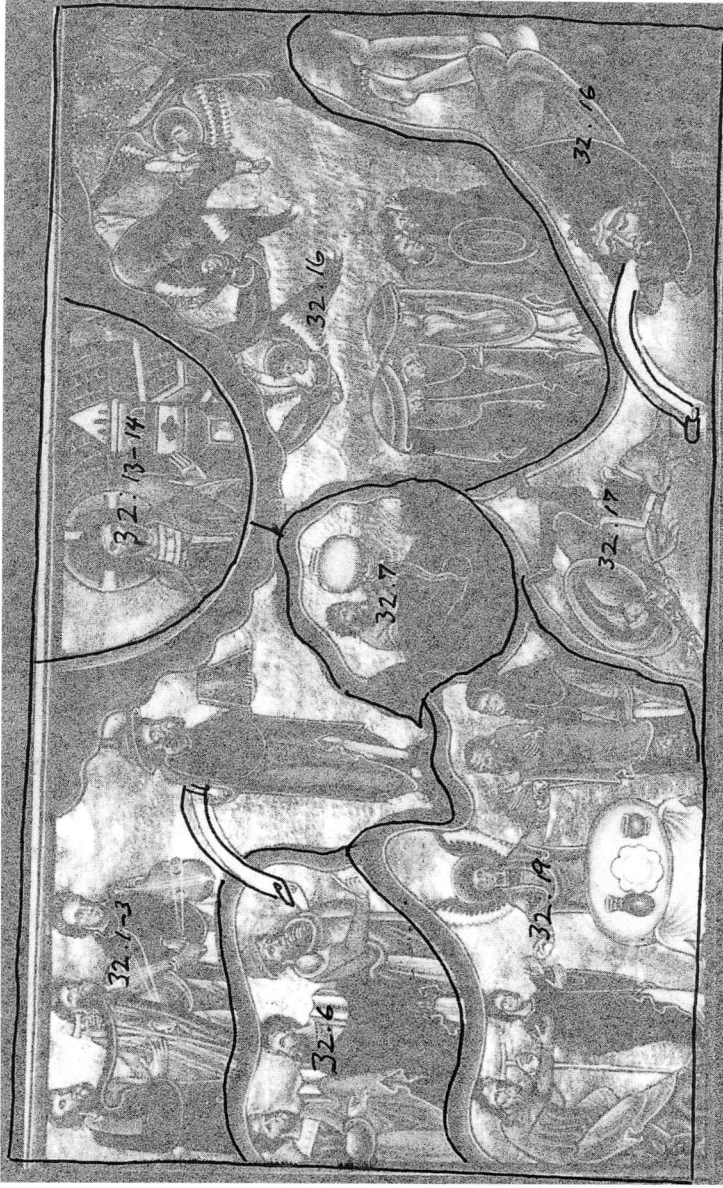

Sandler 21. Paris Psalter, Psalm 32 (with overlay tracing verbal units). Paris, Bibl. nationale MS lat. 8846, fol. 54v (photo from Utrecht Psalter 1996, fig. 19)

Sandler 22. Twyere Psalter, Psalm 7. New York, New York Public Lib. MS Spencer 2, fol. 20
(photo: New York Public Lib.)

Sandler 23. Bohun Psalter, Psalm 79. Vienna Österreichische Nationalbibl. cod. 1826*, fol. 71
(photo: Bildarchiv ÖNB Wien)

Sandler 24. Cuerden Psalter, Psalm 79. New York,
Pierpont Morgan Lib.MS M. 756, fol. 121v
(photo: Pierpont Morgan Lib.)

Sandler 25. Twyere Psalter, Psalm 103. New York, New York Public Lib.
MS Spencer 2, fol. 168v (photo: New York Public Lib.)

Sandler 26. Cuerden Psalter, Psalm 21. New York,
Pierpont Morgan Lib. MS M. 756, fol. 34
(photo: Pierpont Morgan Lib.)

Domine eduxisti ab inferno animam meam: saluasti me a descendentibus in lacum.

Psallite domino sancti eius: et confitemini memorie sanctitatis eius.

Quoniam ira in indignacione eius: et uita in uoluntate eius.

Ad uesperum demorabitur fletus: et ad matutinum leticia.

Ego autem dixi in habundancia mea: non mouebor in eternum.

Domine in uoluntate tua prestitisti: decori meo uirtutem.

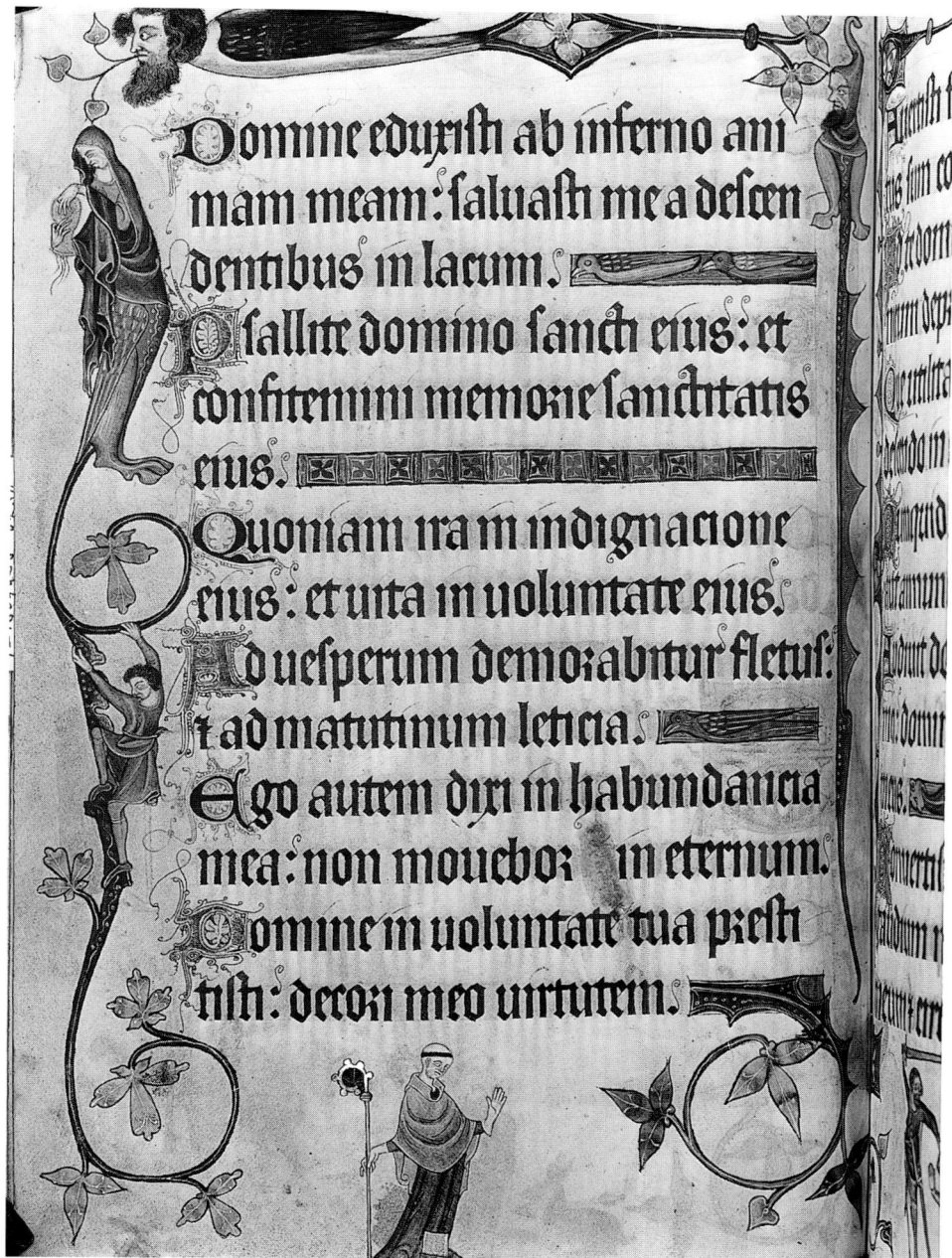

Sandler 27. Luttrell Psalter, Psalm 29. London, British Lib. MS Add. 42130, fol. 55v
(photo: British Lib.)

Sandler 28. Cuerden Psalter, Psalm 41. New York,
Pierpont Morgan Lib. MS M. 756, fol. 64v
(photo: Pierpont Morgan Lib.)

Sandler 29. Paris Psalter, Psalm 41. Paris, Bibl. nationale MS lat. 8846, fol. 72v (from Omont 1906, pl. 49)

Sandler 30. Twyere Psalter, Psalm 40. New York, New York Public Lib.
MS Spencer 2, fol. 73v (photo: New York Public Lib.)